BECOMIN~~~~~~~~~
PAIN IN THE ÄSS

Tom Metzger's first book,
Did Big Brother Give You Permission to Go Wee Wee?
is a great motivational book for reading and talking about.

People know there is something wrong in this country
but just can't figure out what.

Big Brother is written in very easy, understandable language.
It sends a message. It's a wake up call.

It's time to think for yourself, folks, and
stop letting government think for you.
Stop thinking government is the solution when it is the problem.

On the other hand, *Becoming a Political Pain in the Äss,*
the second book, is on *how to do something* about the problems.

The following statement by George Washington gives you all
the information needed to back up what this author is telling you.

> *"Government is not reason; it is force. And force, like fire,
> is a dangerous servant and a fearful master."*
> **—George Washington**

Our government has proven what George Washington
warned us about over 200 years ago.

Now it is time to do something about it.

Also by Thomas F. Metzger:

Did Big Brother Give You Permission to Go Wee Wee?
(ISBN 0-931892-98-8 $12.95, Blue Dolphin)

There is much to learn in the field of activism, and reading this book, written by a man who to date has spent forty years of his life involved as a political activist, will give you some great ideas.

Thomas F. Metzger published a community newspaper for fifteen years, fought battle after battle, and was very effective. If you don't believe this, ask some of his opponents. They will tell you, as much as they didn't like being on the attack end of his pen, they agreed that every community needs someone like him, like him or not.

BECOMING A POLITICAL PAIN IN THE ÄSS

HOW TO
CHANGE
YOUR
GOVERNMENT
SENSIBLY

THOMAS F. METZGER

Blue Dolphin Publishing
1995

Published by Blue Dolphin Publishing, Inc.
P.O. Box 8, Nevada City, CA 95959
Orders: 1-800-643-0765

ISBN 0-931892-99-6

Library of Congress Cataloging-in Publication Data

Metzger, Thomas F., 1936–
    Becoming a political pain in the äss / Thomas F. Metzger.
        p.   cm.
    ISBN 0-931892-99-6
    1. Political participation—United States   2. Political culture—United States.   3. Liberty—Political aspects.   4. United States—Politics and government.   I. Title.
    JK1764.M48 1995
    323'.042'0973—dc20   95-25300
                                                                                  CIP

**WHEN YOU PRONOUNCE THE TITLE OF THIS BOOK,
USE THE BRITISH ENUNCIATION.**
The dots over the "A" in the word ÄSS are called a diacritical mark indicating *umlaut,* which represents a change in the sound of a vowel. In this case, it gives the "A" an "ah" sound. So, with an air of British dignity, give it a bloody good go, and become a real pain in the AHSS.

Cover design: Lito Castro
Text illustrations: Sony

First printing, October 1995

Printed in the United States of America by
Blue Dolphin Press, Inc., Grass Valley, California

10   9   8   7   6   5   4   3   2   1

Table of Contents

Foreword

Here we are less than a year after we published the book titled, *Did Bid Brother Give You Permission to Go Wee Wee?*, and we have another one out. This book is a direct result of the first book. Many people called and wrote, telling me they had read the book, become enthused, but didn't know what to do. Having been an activist most of my adult life, I just was not thinking. I guess I just expected people who read my first book to go out and somehow get involved. This was very presumptuous on my part, and I apologize for that.

In the process of writing this book and reading it before going to press, I realized there are many topics on which I should have expanded in much greater detail, but there is only so much you can say on an issue before it starts to get technical and stuffy. I want you to think for yourself, and you won't if I do it for you.

If you asked fifty activists how to be a political activist, you probably would receive fifty different answers. But if you asked any one of them to outline the major issues a person should learn, know, and understand to be an activist, I believe each would agree that this book has captured those items in a very simple, easy-to-understand format. The intent is to get you to think, so when the time comes that you are ready to get involved, you will have the knowledge and ability to effect change.

In my mind, being a political activist is not something a person does for a month or two and then goes home, jacks up his recliner, and lets the world go by. Activism is something one should learn how to do and then do it for the rest of one's life. There are many levels of activism. There are activities a child can do and some that 100-year-olds can do. In my case, when told by government to obey, I have always rebelled against that "authority" and demanded answers. It has always been a natural process for me to be confrontational with government.

While writing the first book, I should have realized that not everyone is like this. People standing in lines at the post office, store, or bank is one of the best examples of how conditioned people are to do as they are told. Time and again I see people at the head of a line who will not move to the teller or clerk until they are given permission to do so. Lordy, folks, what is the worst thing that can happen if the person at the head of the line just takes it upon himself to think and make a decision to move forward to the teller? I know what I would like to do when they don't move. Don't get me wrong; I'm not saying one should be aggressive—just take a gamble and move forward.

In waiting to start your first political activist activity, compare your actions to a person standing at the front of a line. Are you going to stand there for another decade or so and wait for someone to tell you to move to the counter to pick up your assignment? Or are you going to move on your own and find a project?

If you want to be successful at any endeavor, there is a price to pay. Learn what you have to learn to acquire the knowledge you need to get you where you want to go. If you want to be an effective political activist, use the techniques described in this book. Read the books suggested, collect the information needed, and go to work. You have to take the first step to the counter to pick up your assignment. At the counter of knowledge and success, there is no credit. All life experiences have to be paid in advance.

—T.F.M

Method to My Madness

You MIGHT THINK IT rather strange to buy a book that starts on Chapter 38. Believe me, there is a method to my madness. This is the second book I have written, and I am trying to make it as easy on myself as I can. Since the two books work together as reference books for activists and want-to-be-activists, I thought it would make it much easier if the two books had chapters that run in sequence, so you can refer to chapters, instead of Book One and Book Two, chapter so and so. With my first book, *Did Big Brother Give You Permission to Go Wee Wee?* (hereinafter referred to as the *Big Brother* or *Wee Wee* book), I labored a minimum of six hours a day, seven days a week, for three-and-a-half months. I use the term "labor" in the sense that it is laborious for me to do this. I didn't sweat like many of you good people do in your daily work, but I know what it means to labor ten to twelve hours a day, because I was raised on a farm until I was sixteen years old. Because I was raised on a farm, I also know what it means to be free and have freedom to do the things you want to do.

I was in the Marine Corps at the age of seventeen. By the age of twenty-two or twenty-three, I had started a manufacturing business. At the age of forty, I sold out, moved from the big city to a small, rural town in northern California, bought a newspaper, and began a new career as a muckraking, ass-kicking, limited-government newspaper publisher. Now this is about all you're going to get about my past and what led me to this point in my life. Besides, we are not here to talk about me specifically, even though I occasionally in this book will have to throw in bits and pieces of my life experiences as an activist in order to make a point. Not only that, but when you're reading a book, it is nice to know that the author is not quoting from textbooks he has read but rather has lived and experienced the things he is writing about.

DOING IT WITH CONVICTION

There is one other thing I will say about myself before moving on. I am now and always have been a very intense and dedicated person. When I do something, I put all of my energy into it. When I write or speak about issues in which I am involved, I do it with conviction. I am not writing this book just to be writing a book. I am writing it because I thoroughly believe there will be people who will read it and who will become more deeply involved in the struggle for liberation from our ever more and more oppressive government. I published the aforementioned newspaper for fifteen years with no financial rewards to myself. That is all the proof you need to know that I also live my convictions. The terms "I" and "I am" were over-used in the preceding paragraph only to make a point, not for self-praise. You truly are dealing with someone who is committed, not just involved. In the *Wee Wee* book, I covered the difference between committed and involved. If you've already read it, bear with me, because it needs to be repeated for the people who didn't. It goes like this: When you order steak and eggs for breakfast, the chicken is involved, and the steer is committed. Which are you going to be?

I suspect that my talking to you about doing things with conviction is like the woman who woke up her husband in the middle of the night. She said, "I'm convinced there is a burglar downstairs. Are you going to go down and check it out?" He said, "My dear, I hope that you don't think that I should have the courage of your convictions."

GET THE OTHER BOOK

When I wrote the *Wee Wee* book, I thought it would be the only book I would ever write. As I said before, this is not particularly easy for me. So why am I doing it again, you ask? Well, it's like this. When I wrote the first book, I did it pretty much as a lark. I told my wife we would print 1,000 copies, and if we sold a couple of hundred of them, I could spend the rest my life giving away the balance. It didn't work like that. We printed the first 1,000, and they were gone within four-and-a-half weeks. We ordered a much larger second printing, and I would imagine they will be on the way to being gone by the time this book is finished and printed. You should order the *Wee Wee* book and read it in order to fill in the voids that will be in your mind as you read this book. There is so much to think about in the first book that there is no need to try to recap it in this book. The telephone number and address are on the back page.

D-DAY

As I sit here writing, my wife has the television on, and in the background I can hear them talking about the D-Day celebration. One has to be in awe when one thinks of the suffering, pain, and death that has gone on in the last 200 years in this country in order to acquire, achieve, and preserve freedom. I want you to stop reading for one minute and think about what I just said. ....
.. . .
.... Did you ask yourself what you have done lately to preserve freedom for your children or grandchildren?

WRONG QUESTION

If you asked yourself that question, you asked the wrong question. The real question should be, what have you done in the last week, month, year, or decade to recapture the freedom that we once had? The cry should no longer be for liberty, it should be for liberation from an ever more and more strangling, regulating, controlling, taxing, overpowering, crushing, excessive, fatiguing, and intolerably cancerous, overabundant, big government.

DON'T LIKE TO DO THIS, BUT

In this book I didn't want to reprint or use any of the information from the *Wee Wee* book. But I know that if I don't, then some of you are going to feel lost. I believe that Chapter 6 in the first book is very important in understanding what I mean when I write about our current loss of liberty and compare it to the loss of liberties that our Founding Fathers thought the King of England had taken away from them.

LIBERTY

We will review that chapter in the next chapter, but first get a dictionary and look up the word *LIBERTY*. This word is used several times in the Declaration of Independence and the Constitution and was the motivation of both documents. When you have time, go to your local library or law library and get your hands on a copy of Black's Law Dictionary and look up "liberty." I recommend this because the law dictionary has a more extensive explanation of the term. It is very important to thoroughly understand the legal definition. Looking up the true definition of words is good advice at all times. It eliminates the opportunity for people to double talk you—more on that later.

ARE YOU A FREE MAN???

Pity the poor, wretched, timid soul who is too faint-hearted to resist his oppressors. He has the intellect of a slave. He sings the song of the damned:

"I can't fight back; I have too much to lose; I own too much property; I have worked too hard to get what I have; they will put me out of business if I resist; I might go to jail; I have my family to think about."

Such poor, miserable creatures have misplaced values and are hiding their cowardice behind pretended family responsibility—blindly refusing to see that the most glorious legacy that one can bequeath to posterity is liberty, and that the only sure security is liberty.

THE DECLARATION OF INDEPENDENCE
(Adopted in Congress, July 4, 1776)

Prudence, indeed, will dictate that governments long established should not be changed for light and transient causes; and accordingly all experience hath shown that mankind are more disposed to suffer, while evils are sufferable, than to right themselves by abolishing the forms to which they are accustomed. But when a long train of abuses and usurpations, pursuing invariably the same object evinces a design to reduce them under absolute despotism, *it is their right, it is their duty, to throw off such government, and to provide new guards for their future security.* [Emphasis added.]

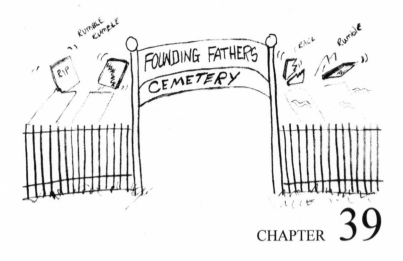

CHAPTER 39

Founding Fathers

ROLLING OVER IN THEIR GRAVES

THIS CHAPTER is a reprint from the *Wee Wee* book. The essence behind both the *Wee Wee* book and this book is the fact that there is basically nothing that we as citizens of the United States of America can do without permission from government or that is not touched directly or indirectly by regulation or taxation. And to more or less prove what I'm saying, I've laid out an overview of the complaints that our Founding Fathers had against the King of England and also a brief list of complaints that we today have against our government. I'm sure if you think about it you can come up with more.

The other day someone said to me that if Benjamin Franklin were alive today he would say, "I can't believe what has happened to the system of government we gave to the people of the United States of America. We never intended for this to happen." When I use the term "founding fathers," I'm usually referring to the fifty-four men who signed the Declaration of Independence and the thirty-nine men who signed the Constitution, but there were many more who were involved.

6

In the great debates surrounding the adoption of the Constitution and the Bill of Rights, life, liberty, property, and the pursuit of happiness seemed to have been important issues in the minds of our Founding Fathers. One need only to read the Constitution and other documents written at the time of the debates to understand this.

THE DECLARATION OF INDEPENDENCE

There are today many patriots in America, but they all pale in comparison to the fifty-four men who signed the Declaration of Independence. These fifty-four men laid on the line their lives, the lives of their families, and their material possessions when they signed their names to the Declaration of Independence. How many patriots do you think would be willing to do this today?

COMPLAINTS AGAINST THE OLD KING

The Declaration of Independence was also about life, liberty, property, and the pursuit of happiness, even though those exact terms were not used. This document listed twenty-seven complaints against the King of England. These complaints ranged from bad laws and coercion to holding meetings in remote places, fatiguing the people into compliance, ignoring the rights of the people, obstructing justice, sending out swarms of military to harass the people, imposing taxes without consent of the people, cutting off trade with the rest of the world, taking away self-rule, plundering the seas, burning towns, and killing our people. These are all issues that are not conducive to life, liberty, and the pursuit of happiness. This is but a brief overview of the complaints they listed. You read the complete document and educate yourself. It is imperative that you do this. You will find it very interesting.

COMPLAINTS AGAINST THE NEW KINGS OF THE U.S.A.

Now let's talk about what our government is doing to us today, 220 years later. On July 4, 1991 we published an article titled, "The Declaration of Liberation" which included the following complaints against our government—all local, state, and federal entities, elected and nonelected officials, politicians, and bureaucrats—today:

1. They have turned our political process at all levels into a battleground of political parties, personalities, and ideologies—and into a vehicle to force their personal beliefs on the citizenry through social planning by the coercive arm of government.
2. They have distorted the Constitution.
3. They have made it so that free people must be licensed to do the most menial tasks for no purpose but government control.
4. They have become pawns to powerful special interest groups.
5. They have passed so many laws that it is impossible to know them all.
6. They have taken away private property rights by dictating what one can and cannot do on one's own property.
7. They have raised taxes to the point that the people are losing their incentive to work.
8. They have taxed every conceivable product.
9. They have taxed and regulated businesses to the point that they can no longer compete in the world market.
10. They have raised the minimum wage so high that they are hurting the very people they profess to be protecting.
11. They have regulated and interfered in the hiring process by passing unfair labor laws, preventing business people from hiring whom they consider most capable.
12. They are passing laws that violate the Second Amendment right to keep and bear arms.
13. They are extorting hard-earned dollars from working people and redistributing that wealth to healthy, able-bodied people who don't want to work.
14. They are forcing businesses to provide child care.
15. They are forcing people to buy insurance and to wear seat belts and helmets.
16. They refuse to enforce the will of the people and carry out the death penalty.
17. They pass gun law regulation to control honest people while being soft on criminals.

18. They have made their careers out of public life.
19. They have passed laws protecting people with deadly diseases such as AIDS, allowing them to roam freely in society.
20. They have bowed to the demands of homosexuals and other minority special interests.
21. They are not protecting our borders from illegal aliens.
22. They are spending money at such a rate it could bankrupt our nation.
23. They have allowed our taxing system to become so complicated that citizens and tax agents cannot interpret it.
24. They have created a bureaucracy so big that the public employees are the most powerful group in America.
25. They have allowed the bureaucracy to become so powerful it can't be controlled.
26. They have passed so many laws that there is nothing a citizen can do without first asking permission of government.
27. They are forcing our free country into a socialist form of government.
28. They pay farmers not to grow crops or to raise livestock.
29. They buy farm products to keep the prices high in the marketplace and then give the products to nonproductive, able-bodied people who don't want to work.
30. They extort millions of dollars from hardworking people to give to foreign countries.
31. They trade votes in order to get millions of dollars for pet, pork-barrel projects in their home districts.
32. They waste billions of dollars through poor management of government.
33. They refuse to heed the warnings and recommendations of professional business people on how to save tax dollars, an example being the Grace Commission Report.
34. They passed laws forcing children to be bused out of their school districts in an attempt to force integration.
35. They refuse to operate within common sense budget restraints, always more concerned about spending money in their district rather than having the best interests of the country at heart.

36. They waste millions of dollars on such projects as the sex life of frogs.
37. They spend millions more on junkets around the world.
38. They pass laws that protect privileged businesses.
39. They have given us a currency that has no real value.
40. They have instituted throughout America hundreds of human service programs, forcing the working people to pay by forced taxation.
41. They have created a welfare system that contains no incentive to get people back to work.
42. They distort the English language by using buzz words and phrases to confuse the masses (doublespeak).
43. They have adopted rent control programs that discourage investors and developers from investing in housing, thereby causing a shortage of affordable housing.
44. They have enacted a tax system that encourages people to have bigger families when overpopulation is a problem, and a welfare system that encourages people to propagate at the expense of the working people.
45. They have passed laws that force people to do things against their will, far beyond the boundaries of good judgment for a government of a free people.
46. They have lost sight of the fact that this country was built on the individual efforts of free people.
47. They have allowed the government school system to become a social experiment instead of a place of basic learning.
48. They continually are forcing their beliefs on the people through taxation.
49. They have made it almost impossible to have freedom of choice and have lost sight of the principles of life, liberty, and the pursuit of happiness guaranteed by the Constitution.
50. They have distorted the meaning of promoting the general welfare, almost to the destruction of America.
51. They have put themselves in the position of playing Caesar over the people; we are again the slaves.
52. They are trying to make all people equal, when in fact free men are not equal, and equal men are not free.

53. They have allowed the I.R.S., C.I.A., F.B.I., and state and local law enforcement to collect reams of information about the private lives of honest, hardworking citizens.
54. They have passed hundreds of laws that serve no purpose but to collect fines.
55. They have passed hundreds of laws that create victimless crimes.
56. They have caused the jails to be filled with citizens who commit victimless crimes.
57. They have passed regulations that violate due process of the law.
58. They have restricted travel through a licensing process.
59. They collect taxes on transactions on which citizens don't earn a profit—for example, on even trade of cars, the D.M.V. collects a tax.
60. They have voted pay increases for themselves and at the same time have raised taxes, which hurt the low-income people the most.
61. They have passed laws forcing pay equality and comparable worth instead of allowing the free market to work.
62. They refuse to reduce the size of government and continually increase it.
63. They have created laws through false dilemmas and contrived crises.
64. They use the power of taxation to practice social engineering, as did Peter the Great, who taxed beards because he didn't like them.
65. They use their positions in high places to do favors for friends.
66. They spend millions of dollars to get elected to a $100,000 per year job.
67. They pass laws that help give preferential treatment to big contributors to elections.
68. They believe they are instilled with more higher knowledge and wisdom than the people, and they think that they alone know what is best for everyone.
69. They have tried to force integration through the passing of a multitude of laws.
70. They have allowed special interest groups to be recipients of tax dollars, special laws, and political favors.

71. They have used affirmative action to give preferential treatment to certain people.
72. They have passed so many laws that they can only selectively enforce them.
73. They have, through the licensing process of television, made broadcasting companies their slaves.
74. They have destroyed, through hundreds of government-funded programs, the incentive to achieve.
75. They have taken the responsibility of care from cradle to grave.
76. They have, for generations and through social programs, allowed healthy, able-bodied people to be nonproductive.
77. They have allowed, with little or no punishment, corruption at the highest levels of government.
78. They are guilty of taking money from the productive and giving to the nonproductive, taking away the incentive to produce.
79. They have promoted a society in which the ambitious are punished by heavy taxes and the lethargic are rewarded with social programs.
80. They have placed the American people in debt for trillions of dollars.
81. They have, through high taxes and regulation, handicapped the entire private enterprise system, reducing incentive and causing inability to compete in a world market.
82. They have passed laws so vague and ambiguous it's difficult to interpret them.
83. They have allowed judges to make laws instead of interpreting and enforcing them.
84. They tax the food we eat through indirect taxes.
85. They have promoted gambling through lotteries to raise funds to quench their thirst for money and power.
86. They have taken the position of moralist to impose their will on the people.
87. They have allowed savings institutions to squander billions of citizens' savings.
88. They are taxing people so heavily that there is talk of a tax revolt.
89. They have allowed government employees' wages and benefits to increase far beyond those of the private sector.

90. They are the largest land owner and own more office space than anyone in the private sector, and they are the largest buyer of goods.

91. They have created a forced retirement program and social security for the private sector, while providing a much better plan for government employees.

92. They have taken money earmarked for social security retirement and spent it on social programs, risking the retirement money of millions of people.

93. They have created a special retirement account for government employees, which is invested to create interest for bigger and better retirement paychecks for them, while social security funds are squandered.

94. They have allowed civil service (military) retirees to collect benefits from three to six times higher than the private sector.

95. They have borrowed so much money that in one year the interest alone is billions of dollars, which has to be paid by the taxpayers.

96. They have allowed street crime to escalate to an unprecedented high.

97. They have all but forgotten the true meaning of the Constitution.

98. They have just recently passed laws that violate the citizens' Fourth Amendment right to be secure in person against unreasonable searches and seizures (asset forfeiture).

99. They have almost invalidated the Ninth Amendment: there are no rights left that are not under government control. You must have permission for most activities.

100. Through social programs, they have eroded the family unit.

101. Through laws, they have restricted the right to work and earn a living in one's own home without a license.

102. They have taxed people so heavily that they are forcing them into government programs with no way out.

103. Because of government regulations and red tape, they have driven up the cost of goods bought by government to a level many times higher than that paid by private sector for similar products.

104. They have, through regulations, made the country a welfare state dependent on government.

105. They have shown a complete lack of confidence in the ability of the American people to solve their own problems.

106. In many cases, they have allowed and promoted democracy (majority rule) to prevail, when history has proven it is the worst form of government; the Constitution guarantees every state in the union a republican form of government.

107. They have violated their oath of office to bear true allegiance to the Constitution.

108. They have, through their actions, shown complete lack of confidence in Americans, similar to communist Russian leaders.

109. They have raised property taxes so high that they are driving people out of homes.

110. Through deception and conniving, they have created a maze of tax upon tax upon tax in order to camouflage the magnitude of the hidden multiple tax burden.

111. They have created a tax code system so complicated that taxing agents give different answers to the same questions.

YOU GOT ANYTHING TO ADD TO THIS?

If you don't have anything to add to this long list, then you are probably in a coma or your name is Gilligan.

SIGN OF GOOD CHARACTER:
THE ABILITY
TO CARRY OUT A RESOLUTION
LONG AFTER THE ENTHUSING HAS WORN OFF.

CHAPTER **40**

What Can You Do?

$\mathbb{A}$FTER READING all the complaints that I listed and adding those that you can up with, topped by years of frustration because of the feeling of total helplessness when trying to deal with government, I would imagine you are ready to put this book in that pile beside or behind your chair and sit on your butt for another decade or two. If you do this, then your children and grandchildren deserve whatever you give them. This is not a very nice way for me to talk to someone who paid good money for my book, but there is no sense in BSing (and that doesn't mean bee-stinging). The cold, hard facts are: as long as you and your friends sit on your asses (and that doesn't mean donkey), nothing in this country will ever change.

SEEN AND NOT HEARD

As you read through this book and we talk about fighting battles, don't lose sight of the fact that not all activists are highly visible people. Many of them are people who work behind the scenes by seeing a problem in their community and quietly going about making the changes. You don't really even know that they are doing their thing, it just gets done. It takes all kinds of people to make communities a better place in which to live, and if all communities better themselves, then America is better. In this book I will try not to get into the liberal and conservative philosophical beliefs too much. I would hope that most people reading this book already understand that it is the liberal, socialist philosophy that is distorting this country. The *Wee Wee* book explains all this.

When you are an activist, you may be in bed with people who have totally opposite political and philosophical views, but who are all working together to accomplish mutual projects. These projects are not particularly political or philosophical; they are community projects. I told several people with whom I was involved in certain projects that they were never to tell anyone that we had sat in the same room plotting strategy to accomplish a mutual mission. It would have tarnished my reputation.

GRASS ROOTS BATTLE

It is going to take a grass roots effort to initiate change in this country, unless, by some miracle, the elected officials of this country wake up and realize that the people can no longer afford our government in such staggering abundance. Government is like a great big fat pig that eats everything in sight and drives the farmer into bankruptcy trying to keep it alive so it can eat more. What we have to do is cut off the fat on our fat pig government. I guess a better way to say this would be to perform liposuction on the big fat pig government. The real function of government has long been lost and forgotten years ago in the shuffle of the bureaucrats' and the politicians' money-feeding-frenzy that has been going on for the last forty to fifty years.

F.D.R.

Seems to me it started right around the time of good old F.D.R. and Eleanor. I had promised myself that I would not bring up their names in this book, and there I go again. You must read in a book by Clarence

B. Carson the true account of what these two did to this country (address below). I will try hard not to mention their names again if you will get this book and read it. This book will give you a better understanding of how the socialist movement really picked up steam in America. Damn, I can hardly stop talking about them. They are like demons from the past, and every time I turn around there they are. I am reminded every time I have to use that damnable social security number. Okay, I'll stop writing for a few moments, take an F.D.R., get a little exercise, and drink a glass of water. I'll be right back. - .

I feel better now. Anyway, we are suppose to be talking about what you can do to help make a difference. Reading the Declaration of Independence and the United States Constitution over and over and over would be the best place to start, as I explain in other chapters. Educating yourself about the history during the F.D.R. period will help you understand from where much of the socialist agenda in America came.

IT'S PHILOSOPHICAL

You need to have this knowledge to understand what it is you're fighting. You're not just fighting to reduce big government; you are fighting the philosophical belief that big government has the solution to our problems. Only knuckleheads believe this. Sorry about that, knuckleheads, but if the hat fits your liberal, socialist, no-logic, shallow-thinking, utopian, daydreaming head, wear it. There are several very good books written by Clarence B. Carson, B.S., M.A., and Ph.D. in history. One of them is *The Welfare State, 1929–1985*, American Textbook Committee, P.O. Box 8, Wadley, Alabama 36276.

Responsibility comes along with kicking government's butt. It's your responsibility to read the right books, associate with the right people, and educate yourself. As you read and have a better understanding of what is really the true function of government, you will see more and more opportunities to attack. You have to learn how to attack, and you have to be prepared to attack when the opportunities avail themselves. A general doesn't send untrained troops into battle, and you should not throw yourself into the political arena without knowledge and understanding. The liberal socialists and the bureaucrats will eat you up. Believe it or not, I will get to the subject of what you can do before the book is finished.

A professor of philosophy asked his friend, "You look depressed. What's the matter?"
His friend replied, "My future."
"So what makes it look so hopeless?" asked the professor.
"My past," said his friend.

CAUTION, DANGEROUS INFORMATION APPROACHING

I use to print in our newspaper information on the activities of patriot and tax avoidance groups. I always printed a headline stating, "Reading this material may be hazardous to your freedom. NOT reading it may be hazardous to your freedom." And I'm telling you right now before you go off half-cocked in trying to mount a frontal attack against a government agency, you had better have your soldiers in line and well trained. Proceed with caution. Don't cause yourself heartburn, unless you are certain that it is going to be well worth it.

The following is part of the F.D.R. legacy, and this is what you are fighting as an activist:

SOCIALIST PARTY, U.S., formed in 1901 by Eugene V. Debs and V.L. Berger out of the Social Democratic Party and a split from the revolutionary Socialist Labor Party, and led for many years by Norman Thomas. It reached its peak in 1912 when, with a membership of 118,000, it got fifty-six socialist mayors and one congressman (Berger) elected while winning 897,000 votes for its presidential candidate (Debs). It opposed U.S. involvement in WWI. In 1919 many radicals left to join the Communist Party. In 1936 right-wing members separated from the Thomas faction to form the Social Democratic Federation, but in 1958 they rejoined, and the party was readmitted to the Socialist International. In 1973 a group led by Michael Harrington split off from the Socialist Party to form the Democratic Socialist Organizing Committee, with the aim of working within the Democratic Party. The Socialist Party candidate for president, David McReynolds, won only 6,720 votes in 1980.

SOCIAL DEMOCRATIC PARTIES, political parties found in many countries that seek socialism through constitutional reform, not revolution. They usually favor government intervention in the economy and nationalization of powerful industries. The Social Democratic Party of the U.S. joined with the Socialist Labor Party in 1901 to form the Socialist Party. In Britain, moderate leaders of the Labour Party broke away to form the Social Democratic Party in 1981.

CHAPTER 41

Getting to Know City and County Government

I NEVER WANT TO TALK DOWN to the readers of any book that I write, so you people who understand a lot about government keep in mind that this book was written with the beginner in mind. After reading my first book, people called and wrote and said, "Now that I'm motivated by reading your book, what do I do?" So comes forth the second book.

Your local City Council and County Board of Supervisors are two very important government entities, and you should become familiar with their functions. I will give you a list of the typical departments that these two boards of elected officials control. I doubt that there are very many differences among the agencies in the cities and counties throughout the country, since most of the these agencies or departments are created by state and federal mandates. If you are a novice at this, you may be surprised at the following long list of departments in our small city and county. Because it takes such huge amounts of tax dollars to operate these agencies, you will all of a sudden begin to realize why so much money is taken out of your paycheck each week.

Multiply these local agencies times all the state and federal agencies and all the other agencies in all the other cities and counties, and you realize why fifty to fifty-five cents of every dollar the working people of this country earn are taken away by government. It cannot continue. It has to change, and you can be a part of that change by educating yourself and becoming involved.

UNBELIEVABLE!!!

The county departments in our small county are: Agriculture, Air Pollution, Animal Control, Area Agency on Aging, Assessor, Auditor-Controller, Board of Supervisors, Building Inspection, Chamber of Commerce, Administration, Building Permits, Environmental Health, LAFCO, Parks & Recreation, Planning, Community Programs, Coroner, County Clerk, County Counsel, Credit Union, Data Processing, District Attorney, Family Support, Elections, Environmental Health, Fairgrounds, Family Support, Farm & Home Advisors/UC Cooperative Extension, Fleet Management, Golden Sierra Job Training Agency, Health Department, Historical Museum, Jail, Juvenile Hall, Law Library, Library, Mental Health, Outpatient Clinic, Psychiatric Health Facility, 24-Hour Crisis Line, Substance Abuse Services, Municipal Courts—Placerville, 495 Main St., & Ponderosa at 3321 Cameron Park Drive, Parks & Recreation, Personnel, Planning Division, Probation, Public Administrator, Public Defender, Public Guardian, Purchasing, Recorder, Risk Management, Sheriffs Department, Superior Court, Surveyor, Transit, Transportation, Treasurer-Tax Collector, Veterans Service Office, and Welfare Department.

Our small city has the following departments: Administration, City Clerk, Finance, Business License, County, Utility Billing, Parking Citations, Public Works, Building Department, Engineering, Planning, Recreation Department, Police Department, and Fire Department.

POOR TAXPAYER

How does all this grab you? And this is a county of only 140,000 people and a city of only about 8,000 people! At one time I discovered there were forty-eight human resource agencies in our little county, all doing what they think needs to be done. The only problem is the poor taxpayer is forced to pay the bill. I say "forced" because I know very few people who would be willing to allow the tax man to remove money from their paychecks so they can have the privilege of going without in order to provide for someone who doesn't particularly want to work and sacrifice to have the necessities of life.

Anyway, get lists from your local government agencies, and look them over. I want you to pretend that you are the self-appointed ruler of your city and county. Ask yourself what changes you would make if you had total control and could do as you wish, keeping in mind that your subjects need certain services in return for the taxes they pay. What would you do to reduce the tax burden for your subjects and at the same time still provide services and prevent tax revolt? How many of the services could be contracted to the private sector? How many laws could you repeal, etc., etc. It is a good mind exercise, and you'll realize that you can come up with solutions for social problems that are just as good as the solutions of any bureaucrat or politician.

"Pay your taxes with a smile," said the accountant to his distraught client.
"I wish they would accept that," said the client.

DON'T BE OVERWHELMED

Don't let all of this overwhelm you. How do you eat an elephant? One bite at a time. Find a government activity that upsets you, then research and find out why and how that certain department was set up. You might be surprised to find out that there are departments which are truly no longer needed but which are just never abandoned. To dismantle a government agency is not the place for a novice to start. The point here is for you to get acquainted with the workings of local government.

As you contemplate the long list of departments in your local government, you might ask yourself what really would happen if a certain agency were done away with. Too many people have been conditioned to think that we can't survive without all this government we have. You might be surprised and come to the conclusion that ninety-five percent of the people would never even know if a certain government agency closed its doors for the next six months. Of course, there are a few legitimate functions for government. We just do not need nor can we afford to pay for the abundance of government that we have today.

CAREER POLITICIANS

The phenomenon of career politicians is one reason for our runaway, overburdening government. Some of the have been in Washington so long that they have lost touch with reality. They don't live in the real world. They don't even have to live by the very laws they pass. They have pay scales and benefits unequal to those of the working people. It is your job to sort out these ideas and motivate yourself into action.

DONUT-SHOP POLITICIAN

It might be fun to be a donut-shop politician, but you sure as hell won't accomplish much. As a matter of fact, it use to anger me when I went around on Fridays putting papers in some of the businesses in town, listening to people bitch and moan about government. When I would suggest something they could do, they always had an excuse why they couldn't do it. Some who were in business were afraid of losing business, calling attention to themselves, causing someone to come after them, or having trouble with the I.R.S. As a matter of fact, I just looked in the *Wee Wee* book and on page 6, Chapter 2 there is a very good saying about this, titled, "Are You A Free Man?" It might insult you, so if you are thin-skinned, don't bother reading it.

GET ON THE STREET

By being on the street at least once a week, I was able to have an edge on the other paper in town, because the publisher of the other paper never left his computer hole except to go to his tea party functions (service clubs) with his political friends. When they needed to be told on, he couldn't do it. If you decide to try pamphleteering or publishing a small newspaper, you can't have political friends. Your job is to tell the public everything that you discover. If you want to know what people are thinking and what they want to know, you have to be on the street and be a good listener. You need to learn how government works and pass it on to other people. If you decide to get motivated and become an activist, you will be among a select group of patriots. It doesn't take a big percentage of the people to make changes; as a matter of fact, throughout history it has always been a very small, select group of activists who have been responsible for many of the changes. Many of the people involved in an activist movement are in it for a variety of reasons. But somewhere behind the scenes, there will be a master mind helping and guiding the actions of the group. This person usually is well-informed on the types of issues I am presenting in this book. The object of this book is not only to train you to get out and fight battles but to educate you so you will be an effective leader and thinker and will be able to motivate other people to become involved.

TRUER TODAY THAN THEN

"You cannot bring about prosperity by discouraging thrift. You cannot strengthen the weak by weakening the strong. You cannot help the wage earner by pulling down the wage payer. You cannot further the brotherhood of man by encouraging class hatred. You cannot help the poor by destroying the rich. You cannot keep out of trouble by spending more than you earn. You cannot build character and courage by taking away man's initiative and independence. You cannot help men permanently by doing for them what they could and should do for themselves."

—Abraham Lincoln

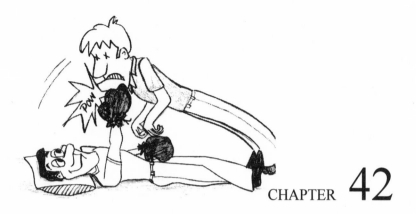

Fighting From
the Bottom Up

MAKE CHANGES in your own community! If every community in America were made ten percent better, America would be ten percent better. How do you eat an elephant? You eat it one bite at a time. Remember this statement and don't forget it. Time after time I have seen people who think they are going to change the entire system. This won't happen in this lifetime or the next. If you have done as I have told you and read the Declaration of Independence, and you've read it to try to find some answers, you should have noticed that our Founding Fathers were right once again. They said, and let me quote, "Prudence indeed, will dictate that governments long established should not be changed for light and transient reasons, . . ."

When you take on the government, you have to choose your fight with care, and even then you could end up like a boxer I heard of:

After five hard rounds, the boxer goes back to his corner, bruised and bloody, and the manager says, "You're doing great, he hasn't laid a hand on you."

The boxer said, "If he hasn't laid a hand on me, then you better keep an eye on the referee, because someone is beating the hell out of me."

THE LONG TERM???

Think about what that means and what the Founding Fathers had in mind the next time you want to try to change some function of government. Your notion might sound like a good idea at the moment, but think of the long-term effects of what it is you are trying to change. Also, ask yourself if it someday is going to come back and bite you in the ass.

Example: A barber had his shop in a shopping center, and he was enjoying a very good business. He one day discovered that there was another barber who wanted to open another barber shop in the same shopping center. The old barber had a friend on the City Council. He went to him and somehow convinced him to introduce an ordinance allowing only one barber shop in each shopping center. It passed by a three to two vote and became law. The old barber was happy and the potential competitor had to go elsewhere. A few years later, the old barber decided to retire and travel. Returning after two years, he became bored and decided to go back into business. However, all the good locations in the shopping centers were taken. His own law bit him in the ass.

The point here also is not so much that you are going to do something that will bite you in the ass personally, but you might do something that will come back to haunt your children and grandchildren. You see, this is what our elected officials have been doing for years. They pass laws for self-interest, as was done for the barber.

LEARN, LEARN, LEARN

Educate yourself and be knowledgeable in whatever area of government you choose to involve yourself. Start learning the process.

For example: if you want to take on your local Planning Department, ask for a copy of the ordinances which dictate how they operate. This is very important, because you might be upset with a government employee, thinking that he's way off base on a certain decision or issue. However, after reading the ordinance, you will probably find that nine times out of ten they were following the rules. If a government employee does something wrong, realize that before you can have any recourse against him, you have to prove malice, proving that whatever he did was done intentionally to harm you. That, my friend, is almost impossible to prove, unless you have a witness who will testify that the employee set out to harm you.

BY THE BOOK

I realize that I'm talking about subjects you can't do anything about, but you have to know these things up front or you will waste a lot of time running around accomplishing nothing. And understand that most everything that government employees do is done by the book. If they don't do it by the book, they get in trouble. As I said before, there are ordinances which give them the authority to do what they do, so don't get angry with the employee. Check the law, and if the law is bad, then get yourself involved.

They do their work by the book. If you don't like the way they do things, go about getting the rules changed. Government workers are pretty much comprised of non-risk-takers. They have learned over the years that the way to keep their job is to follow the rules. Then, if something goes wrong, it is not their fault. When a problem arose in a government agency thirty years ago, they made a new rule to take care of it. They continue to make new rules all the time, but they never delete any of the old ones; therefore, they have this tremendous set of rules that the bureaucracy has to live with.

HOW NOT TO FAIL IN GOVERNMENT

People in government have learned that the only way not to fail is not to do too much. If they see something wrong with the system, they don't try to change it. They just work within the system so they will keep their jobs. If a government employee ever gives you a blank look when you ask him to use a little common sense regarding a problem, you'll know you're dealing with a well-seasoned veteran who doesn't want to lose his job. The point is, if you know and understand this, it will make your job easier, because you will attack the problem in the right place—the rule book, not the employee.

THERE ARE THOSE WHO DON'T KNOW, AND
THERE ARE THOSE WHO DON'T KNOW
THEY DON'T KNOW.

CHAPTER 43

Getting Acquainted with Your Controllers

ONE OF THE FIRST THINGS you need to do is to get acquainted with the people who control your life. And this doesn't mean that you have to introduce yourself at this point unless you are just getting into the battle mode of a certain issue. Your objective at this point is to get acquainted with the names of your elected officials and the department heads (bureaucrats). Employees are not usually classified as bureaucrats. Keep in mind, the people you need to know are the ones who make and enforce the laws. Don't waste your time dealing with the employees unless they are employees who are willing to feed you information when you need it. And believe me, they will do this if they trust you never to disclose your sources. More on that in another chapter.

GET A LIST

Call your City Hall and county level offices. They should have lists of all the elected officials and department heads. While you're at it, call your state elected official and request a list of all the state elected officials. If you have a good conservative representative, ask him to identify other good conservatives, the conservatives who believe in less government. At this point, don't waste your time getting a list of state departments or agencies. As a matter of fact, keep your nose out of state and federal affairs until you have gone through your apprenticeship training at the local level. Better yet, always mind your own business at home first, tending to local city and county issues.

DON'T GET MAD, GET EVEN

While publishing my newspaper, people time after time called me or came to me depressed, sad, and angry about something that had been done to them by government. The first words out of their mouths were, "I'm going to see to it that I get fired the s.o.b. who did this to me, and I'm going to fight government from now on."

Well, they probably won't get the s.o.b. fired, and they more than likely will fight only one battle with government, and that will be their own. Ninety-nine percent of the time these people don't even know if there is a law giving the government the power to do what they do. Don't get me wrong. Even if there is a law, it doesn't mean the law is a good law, and laws can be changed—more about this in another chapter. The point here is to put your anger to good use—to get you off your ass and into action. Hopefully it will stoke your determination to hang in there for the duration.

A man is ready to walk out the door to go to work when his wife asks him to go into the kitchen and give the maid hell. "Why do you want me to do that?" he asked. "She's been doing a good job."

"Because she is going to beat the rugs today, and she does a better job when she is angry."

LONG WAY TO GO

I suppose you think you're ready to go fight a battle, now that you know who the players are. Well, not hardly. If you are at this moment hell bent to go fight a battle, this book is not going to stop you. This book is not a quick solution to any problem. If you are a novice, if anything it will slow you up for awhile but hopefully help you in the long run by making you more effective when you do get involved.

GET PREPARED

You should have separate telephone and address books for the names of political activists and government offices. I found that I prefer to have two separate books or three-ring notebook binders and paper. Papers can be moved around more easily within a three-ring notebook binder and, if you're like me and have more than one battle going at one time, the tabbed dividers make it much easier to remain organized. You should list separately the people in city government from those at the county, state, and federal offices. Keep all the agencies separate, too. Then, if you start a battle with county government, you can either move the list of names and phone numbers to the section you have set up for the battle, or run a copy of the list, punch the holes in it yourself, and place it in your action section. As time goes on, you will find that your list of names will become invaluable. It might be smart always to have a duplicate set of all the names and numbers. Put into categories your list of political allies according to talents and types of battles they will fight. Don't take this hint lightly, because if you stay involved it will save you lots of time in the long run.

NOTHING HAS CHANGED

Confucius was China's most famous teacher, philosopher, and political theorist. His ideas have influenced the civilization of all of eastern Asia.

Confucius was born in 551 BC and orphaned at an early age. Although largely self-educated, he became the most learned man of his day. He was deeply disturbed by the social conditions of his time, and dedicated his life to social reform. His primary emphasis was on sincerity, and his whole teaching was based upon ethics. **He believed that government should make its end not the pleasure of the rulers but the happiness of their subjects.**

*"To put the world right in order, we must first put the nation in order; to put the nation in order, we must first put the family in order; to put the family in order, **we must first cultivate our personal life;** we must first set our hearts right."* [Emphasis added.]

NOTHING HAS CHANGED

CHAPTER 44

Keeping the Controllers in Check

In the State of California we have what is known as the Brown Act. This is a law that makes sure the politicians perform all of their functions in open public forums. In California the law is published by the Attorney General's Office, and I would imagine it is the same in most states. If you live in another state, get a copy of the law that regulates the conduct of your elected officials. I'll give you some examples of the types of restrictions in California. By the way, this law not only governs the elected officials but is far-reaching and covers any body that is appointed and assembles to discuss public business.

QUORUMS

For this discussion we will be talking about elected or appointed groups of five members. On a board of five, there have to be three present to make a quorum to vote on issues. The Brown Act makes it illegal for three members to be in the same place at the same time

33

discussing any public business. All public business is to be conducted in an open public forum duly convened to do business. All public meetings have to be publicized, so that interested citizens can be present to give input if they so desire. Have you ever been to a public meeting and heard them adjourn to go into closed session? This also is regulated. Prior to adjourning, they must announce what it is they are going to discuss in the closed session. It is usually restricted to personal matters, lawsuits, land purchases, and the like. What can be discussed is narrowly defined. Most all public bodies have an attorney who is present at all meetings to make sure the elected officials stay within the law. But don't ever think this is a foolproof situation. Get a copy of the public meeting law in your area, study it, and then keep an eye on them. If you don't want to go to meetings, get the agenda packets and monitor their actions. Once they have committed an offense, you can nail them anytime. Everything on which the public bodies vote is recorded in the minutes, so you can look back days, weeks, or years to see who voted for what on any issue. You can also go back to check how a certain person voted on all past issues. This can reveal a lot about an elected official and makes good fodder for hot and heavy political campaigns, or you can use it to your candidate's advantage.

SERIAL CALLS

They cannot make what is defined as "serial" phone calls—one member calling the other members to get a consensus as to how they are going to vote. They can't make conference phone calls with other members. There is much more but I don't have room to detail it all. The point is, if you know these things you can become a very effective watchdog for your community. Over the years I nailed the City Council and the County Board of Supervisors for violations of the Brown Act. You too can learn to become a real political pain in the ass.

As you get into this idea of being a watchdog, you will not only find it very interesting, but you will become very effective in making changes in your community. You noticed I said "in your community." Keep your nose out of state, federal, and world affairs, and work on issues in which you can be effective. But you have to get smart, work smart, and pick and choose your battles.

This area we just discussed is important, because you can help keep government on the straight and narrow by using their own laws. As a matter of fact, almost everything you do as a activist will have something to do with the law. Remember, everything that government is allowed to do is in writing, and it is supposed to be followed. If it is not followed, it is at this point that the alert watchdog can step in and put government back in line. You also can analyze the law, and if it needs to be revised or eliminated, you can set about doing that.

ICE COLD STEAM

The following quote is attributed to three people—John Philpot Curran, Wendell Phillips, and Thomas Jefferson: "Eternal vigilance is the price of freedom." Let me tell you, folks, no truer words have ever been spoken. It would be nice to think that our elected officials were looking out for our best interests, but this is like asking for ice cold steam. Once these people are in office, something happens to their thinking process, and this is where the activist patriot can come into play. It is your job to keep them on their toes. It's time for you to be a real pain in the ass.

GET THEM WITH THEIR OWN RULES

Familiarize yourself with your city and county ordinances. These are the rules especially for city or county. These not only have the rules for elected officials but the rules for the city manager and the department heads as well. The same can be said for the county, except that the person who manages under the elected board is entitled County Administrative Officer (C.A.O.). As an example, in our city government there was an elected official who thought he was indispensable and hung out at the City Hall just about every day telling people what to do. We researched the city ordinance. It very clearly stated that it was the function of the City Manager to run the day-to-day operation of the city, and he was to take his orders from the entire elected body during open public sessions. I can't say that we put a stop to the antics of this one particular elected official, but we called enough attention to his activities over the years that it hindered his operation. By the time I had bought the newspaper, he had already been in office almost ten years and had established himself as the dictator of the community. This little man was his own one-man operation. He was able to have people fired, and he moved employees from department to department so they could be his informants. Most every city has a guy like this, so keep your eyes open.

MINI MAFIOSO

The voters finally got fed up with his dictatorial attitude and Mafioso style of politics and booted him out. I would like to take some of the credit for informing the public of his actions and his not being re-elected. The main point here is, if you are going to be a watchdog, make sure that you keep close tabs on your local elected officials, because in most smaller communities they tend to be trusted too much. Never trust politicians, or you will be like the family pet who becomes familiar with the people who come and go from the house, and then one day someone walks off with the family jewels while the dog is sleeping by the front gate. It is not that this little man I am talking about was doing such bad things for the city. He in fact did almost nothing. He refused to play by the rules. The only way for the people to keep control of their government is to have all public business conducted and documented in open public meetings. This little dictator's biggest problem was he had no public communication skills, so he operated behind the scenes in the dark of night to accomplish what he thought was best for the City.

If you have a person like this in your community, immediately expose everything they do. Don't allow them to continue to operate as such, because it is not in the best interest of the community. The object of representative government is not to allow any one person to be in control. And when public business is conducted in public, a dictatorial-type personality most of the time is kept in line by the other elected officials. I said "most of the time." At other times it is up to an alert political activist to do his job.

The barber in a small town asked his customer why he always talked about the weather. The man answered, "You don't expect me to talk about our local City Council while you are shaving me with a razor, do you?"

As Justice William O. Douglas, speaking for the United States Supreme Court, stated:

"The concept of the public welfare is broad and inclusive. . . . The values it represents are spiritual as well as physical, aesthetic as well as monetary. It is within the power of the legislature to determine that the community should be beautiful as well as healthy, spacious as well as clean, well-balanced as well as carefully patrolled."

FINE CHINA

CHAPTER 45

Take It Easy

WHEN YOU WANT to make a change, you have to know the ropes. Know the system and work smart to accomplish your goal. This doesn't mean that you can't go headlong into a battle with no experience and be victorious, because you can. It just saves a lot of time and heartburn if you have some idea how to go about it. If you go in like a bull in a china closet, the people whose help you want sometimes will resist helping because of your attitude and aggressiveness. LEARN TO STAY CALM. Don't get angry. When you get angry you lose credibility, and you don't think straight. You also have to go into these battles with the knowledge that it takes time, and it should.

SLOW AND EASY

Does it shock you when I say that it should take time? There will be times when you will say to yourself, "This law is so stupid; a child could see that it needs to be fixed or repealed." Our Founding Fathers said in the Declaration of Independence, "Government should not be changed for light and transient reasons." Think of the huge demonstrations of the past when people didn't like a certain law and wanted a change. Never have I seen government call a special session to pass or repeal a law to satisfy a mob. If every time someone wanted a new law or an old law changed or repealed, can you imagine the chaos that would follow if the elected officials obliged? Look at the mess this country is in as you read this. There are now so many laws, no knows what they are.

GETTING STARTED

You can make a very effective beginning as a watchdog at the local level by getting copies of the City Council and County Board of Supervisor meeting agenda. All you have to do in most counties and cities is simply request that a copy be sent to you. Some government agencies charge for this service, but it is usually a minimal charge of around $50.00 per year. If it is much more than this, then you might have your first battle carved out for you. Government agencies are not supposed to charge more than their cost for any services. So if the agenda costs more than ten cents per page plus mailing cost, ask them why. The agenda gives you a very good overall view of local government activities. If you don't know what your local government is doing, then you sure as hell should not be sitting around the lunch room or coffee shop talking about state, federal, and world affairs, should you? If you want to be a real pain in the ass, you have to know where to stab.

IT'S NO ACCIDENT

Always remember that nothing in government happens by accident. Almost everything that happens in government has to go through discussion and debate in a public meeting and be approved by your elected officials. As much as the system seems screwed up, it works fairly well considering all things. I have thought about this system and tried to invent my own, but I always come up with a malevolent dictatorship. And it would work fine if I were in charge; you know what I mean. Just for a little mind exercise, you think about it and see what you come up with. Keep in mind that representative government has its flaws. But if individual rights are of the highest priority, there is not much choice as far as governments go. Government is one of those necessary evils. There are controls but not enough patriots to keep government in check. People have to take charge and run their government, or the government, by nature, will run the people.

Speaking of accidents, Dick asked Jane if she had ever been in a train accident.
"Yes," she said, "once when I rode a train."

SERVANTS PAID BETTER THAN US

This is where we are today as a nation. We are totally controlled by our servants in this country. This is a strange situation. The servants of the people earn more and have better benefits than the people who pay their wages. Don't let anyone in government tell you that they pay taxes, because they don't. We people in the profit sector pay a double tax every time a government employee pays tax. We pay the tax that pays the wages of the government employees; therefore, when they pay tax, they pay with our tax money. Don't ask me for a solution to this problem. The only solution seems to be to reduce the wages of the government employees by the amount of tax they should pay. At least that way the tax man is not taking the money away from the people in the profit sector where it can be used in the marketplace. There are many interesting ideas to think about, ideas I consider thought-provoking, stimulating, and entertaining, but they don't accomplish too much.

The following is Webster's Dictionary definition of bureaucracy:

bu•reau•cra•cy *n.* 1. the administration of government through departments managed by officials following an inflexible routine 2. the officials collectively 3. governmental officialism or inflexible routine 4. concentration of authority in a complex structure of administrative bureaus

bu•reau•crat *n.* an official in a bureaucracy, esp. one who follows a routine strictly, insisting on proper forms, petty rules, etc.

bu•reau•cra•tize *vt., vi.* to make or become bureaucratic

As you can see, it says a bureaucracy is managed by officials following an inflexible routine. I never really thought about it like that, but it is obvious that this inflexibility would be one of the biggest problems that we could have in this country of free spirits. I use that term loosely. It is a matter of spirit whether we are free spirits anymore or not. Anyone who is a free spirit is a very flexible individual who wants to come and go and do as they please. And when a free spirit has to deal with an inflexible government bureaucracy, it is obvious there is going to be friction. There are no laws, rules, regulations, or policy that can fit any one situation, but by Webster's definition the fact that bureaucracy is inflexible creates a big problem.

PPPPPPPPP Words

Pᴏʟɪᴛɪᴄɪᴀɴs, polling place, philosophy, press, power, pressure, political pain, people, pencil, photography, parades, picket, protest and pamphleteering:

THE P-WORDS

TOOLS

There are several tools of the trade of the Constitutional Patriot Activist (C.P.A.), and I refer to them as The P-Words. The P-Words are the tools you have to learn to use and apply in your new trade as a C.P.A. You have to learn when and how to apply each of them to your advantage to accomplish your mission. If you're going to be a C.P.A., learn your trade, study, know what you're doing, and understand the Constitution. Don't use the power of The P-Words indiscriminately and get yourself in trouble.

Throughout this book I will talk about all The P-Words, but in this chapter we will try to define each activity to stimulate your mind into action. Think about using these tools in the battle against the cancerous, over-regulating, and controlling government. You cannot allow yourself to be lulled into a false sense of security thinking there is nothing wrong in America today. People fool themselves into believing that everything is OK because they still have enough money to buy food for the week and pay the rent. In the *Wee Wee* book, I challenged people to name ten activities a person can do that are not touched by taxation or regulation. You can't do it, and so that means government somehow has managed to gain almost total control of your life and the lives and future lives of your children and grandchildren. Is this what you want for your posterity? If it is, you shouldn't waste your time reading this book or the *Wee Wee* book. You might as well forever be a couch potato and wait for the end or the daily rule book analogy I predicted in the *Wee Wee* book. Or you can get off your knees and on your feet and do something, even if it is wrong.

MISSION FIRST

The object in most of my writing is to get you to think. Don't expect me to have all the answers. If you do not think for yourself, you will always be a less effective citizen and activist. In the following explanations of The P-Words, let your imagination go to work. Think how you can use any one of The P-Words to accomplish a mission.

Politicians This seems to be the key to most of our problems, but doing something about them is almost an impossibility. You can write letters to them and you can plead with them, but most of them only respond to the threat of not being re-elected. On a local level, you can be effective working in election campaigns to elect the right people into office. This means voting for people who believe less government is the best government, have read the Constitution, understand what it means, and will carry out their oath of office to bear true faith and allegiance to the Constitution. It is your job to make them do this.

Politics This is an area you have to study and understand. Understand that America evolves around politics. This is what I mean when I say that government has complete control of your life through taxation and regulation. Webster's definition of politics is: having particular wisdom; crafty; unscrupulous; artful. Now you know what you are dealing with. You have to realize that you are dealing with people who have an agenda. It's up to the people of this country to change the direction of politics—from an out-of-control government to one that is under control and from a liberal socialist agenda to liberty and freedom once again. Use your head and ask yourself how you can be effective in the battle.

It is a shame, but I am coming closer and closer to believing that my friend and neighbor might be accurate in his statement, "All it takes to be a politician is to have no self-respect." This is a shame, isn't it?

Polling Place   When it comes time to vote in your community, get out there and form alliances with like-thinking people. Work hard to make a difference IN YOUR COMMUNITY. It is great sport to talk about the race for the presidency and state and federal offices, but from where do most of these people come? They come from the minor leagues—the local level. Many times a good old boy at the local level gets elected because he or she will repair a street, fill a pothole, vote in a certain subdivision, or maybe put a certain individual on a commission of some kind or another. If we work at electing people with the right philosophical beliefs at the local level, we will accomplish two things: first and most important, we will make changes in community politics; and second, if they gravitate to the top and their minds are not corrupted on the way up, we will have a few proper-thinking people at the top level.

Philosophy   There is nothing more vital than your making it your business to know the philosophical beliefs of your elected officials or the people who are running for public office. Never be fooled by what a politician says or even by what he or she does. People with deep philosophical beliefs will say and do most anything to accomplish their philosophical mission in life. It should be apparent to you by now, unless you are in a coma, that the agenda of the liberal, socialist, far-left-thinking people is for more socialism in America. The far left are becoming sensitive to being called socialists. After the fall of the Communist party, even the socialists are embarrassed to be associated with the socialist agenda. On the television program that I do weekly, three or four liberal co-hosts have fallen by the wayside. They couldn't handle, week after week, the heat of having their no-logic, shallow thinking exposed. One host told me that people told him that Metzger really made him look bad. I told him I didn't make him look bad, his philosophical beliefs made him look bad.

SLIPPERY PEOPLE

Know as much as possible about the inner thoughts of the people in office who represent you. This will give you a good idea of what they are going to do on any certain issue even before they do it. Politicians are slippery, but they are usually fairly true to their deep philosophical beliefs. They might dance around and do things that at the moment seem to be counterproductive to their true agenda, but somehow it will benefit them in the end. It is kind of like the communist philosophy of taking two steps forward and one step back. While it looks like they are stepping back, they have actually taken one step forward. How do you find out how politicians think? Simple—make an appointment and ask them questions. Better yet, write them a letter and get their response in writing. There's nothing a politician hates worse than this. Write your letter, as I suggest in another chapter, by the numbers. Ask them what are their three favorite books. Ask them if they were President and could do anything they wanted to do for the people, what would they do? Find out who are three of the politicians in history and three of the present day politicians they admire and respect. If they say their favorite book is by Lenin, and if they were President they would make sure that everyone had everything they needed, and their favorite politician is Ted Kennedy, you have some real problems. Do you see what I mean? If your representatives don't want to respond to your questions, find other ways of obtaining the information. It really is important to know how your political opponents think. You also will discover your allies in this process.

Press   Know the people who write for your local papers. Find out how they stand on political issues. If they are smart they will say they are neutral and have no position. Well, this is usually BS. They have opinions on most issues, and it shows in their writing. You can tell by the headlines how the powers to be at the newspaper stand on issues. If they use very aggressive-type headlines on an issue they are reporting, it usually means they are on the attack. On the other hand, if that same story in another newspaper is buried in the back of the paper, it also tells you something doesn't it? Pay attention, folks. People emit continual little signals; you just have to be alert and look for them. You can find out the political leaning and how biased a newspaper is by watching the letters to the editor. You can learn this real fast by you and your friends writing some letters to the editor which contain different political slants. Notice which ones they print. The point is, in addition to understanding your politicians, know and understand your local newspapers, radio, and television stations.

Power   Know where the power base lies in your community. Believe me, there will be one, because it seems to be human nature for certain people to gravitate toward power and control, a phenomenon to which I referred in the *Wee Wee* book. You have to know who these people are or you might play right into your oppositions' hands by saying the wrong things to the wrong people. Understand that certain people thrive on power—the power of their positions by being able to make things happen for people and the kind of power that allows them to have control over people.

Pressure   If you learn and understand your subjects, knowing where and how to apply pressure will come naturally. I know a politician who was hanging around the wrong places and was seen by a law enforcement officer in a car with a young lady. Since the deputy was off duty, he didn't do anything about it but told me about it in confidence. This politician was thinking about running for re-election, so I made a phone call to him and embellished the story a mite. Lo and behold, he decided not to run. I also told him that I had proof that he had been having breakfast with a gentleman on a regular basis who was paying for his meal and turning the slip into the county for food allowance. He decided not to run for re-election; case dismissed. One of the most powerful tools is being the only one who has dirt on someone in government. So don't be too quick to give up that kind of information to the general public or even to your best friend. Information is power only if no one else has it. You and you alone can then barter with it. Don't try to blackmail anyone; it's against the law. Make political deals.

Political Pain This category goes hand in hand with the above paragraph, "Power," in the sense that if you have dirt on someone you can use it to apply political pain. Again, you have to use your imagination on these issues. All cases are different. You have to figure out what will cause pain to your targeted representatives in your area. Some politicians are so entrenched that they don't give a damn what anyone says about them. They will find a way to skate free. There are a multitude of P-Word activities that will cause political pain. Use your head and scheme but use the Constitution as your guide.

People Learn to use, not abuse, people; you help me and I'll help you; you scratch my back and I'll scratch yours. Learn how to organize and motivate people to accomplish a mission. Rally them to public meetings to protest or support a certain project, always keeping in mind to use good judgment. Don't rally, protest, or support only for your benefit and self-interest, because it discredits you. "People power" in meetings is very effective.

Pencil The pen is mightier than the sword, and so is the pencil. It is just like it says on the front page of this book, "The Ultimate Weapon." Use it with caution, because it can come back and bite you in the butt. Go to your local law library and look up "libel" and know what it means. Writing letters to the editor is a safe place to start because, if they are on the ball, they will edit your letter, and if you have gone over the line and have written something that is libelous, they simply will not print it. If a newspaper prints your letter and it is libelous, they are the ones who are sued right along with you, because they passed on the information and they should know better. Letter writing to elected representatives has some effect, but not much unless you are writing to your local elected officials. There it can have some effect because they will feel the heat from the local people who read your letter to the editor. Your letter can be especially effective if you make your letter public or send copies to the right people. Make sure the politician to whom you are writing knows that you are sending copies of the letter to other people. Of course, you can always give them the benefit of the doubt on the first letter by mailing it to them and waiting for a response.

Photography   This is a great way to record events and document attendance. If you are alert, you will get some nice pictures that you can keep on file for future use. At all times keep your eyes open. Nowadays, with the great little point-and-shoot cameras, you can at all times have one on a lanyard around your neck when you are at public functions or out doing your daily duties. When in doubt, shoot, and keep it on file. One never knows. On several occasions I took a good camera with a telephoto lens and sat in on public hearings, keeping my camera trained on some arrogant S.O.B. elected official who had tried to give me a bad time. All during the meeting I would shoot pictures, sometimes catching him in positions such as picking his nose or having a dumb look on his face. I then would use that picture in my newspaper, quoting some profound statement he had made during the meeting. If you do this, you will feel the tension right through the camera lens.

LITTLE MAN, BIG GUN

Someone told me that a city council member (our little Mafioso man) was laying a gun on the council table behind a little partition. So, during the meeting, I got up, walked behind the table, and shot a picture of the man and his gun before he even knew what happened. The headline read, "PISTOL PACKING POLITICIAN," and the picture showed a very angry politician with his gun. The end result was that he no longer brought a pistol to the meetings. Nothing is more convincing than a photograph for the public to see. Many times you don't even need a story, just a small caption. On one occasion, someone told me that one of the board members of our local water district was sleeping during meetings, so I took my trusty camera and went to the meeting right after this person had returned from lunch. Sure enough, he was sound asleep within fifteen minutes. I walked up within four feet of him and took half a dozen pictures. The caption on this picture was, "While he snoozes, the rate payer loses." He was angry, but it didn't seem to interrupt his sleep.

LOOK AT ALL THE GOVERNMENT

We drove around the county and took pictures of all the government buildings and printed them in the paper. People were shocked. They had no idea the size of government in our small county. Prior to this, I had written articles about it, but the fact alone had little impact. The point was driven home with the pictures. Another time we took pictures of all the equipment at the Department of Transportation and printed how much it had cost the taxpayers. The courtroom is another good source of pictures. If you can convince the court that you have a newspaper or are working for one, you can go into court with permission and document who is involved in government cases. With high speed film you can shoot pictures in public places having low light, places where the local politicians hang out, you know what I mean. Bad pictures of politicians are great to have at election time. Don't forget this. If you are going to play, play to win. Go to your local Police or Sheriff's Department and ask for a press pass. It is usually good for a year and opens doors for you. Try telling them that you are a free-lance photographer. You might want to order a business card stating that you are a free-lance reporter and photographer. You'll find out how easy it is to get into places if you carry a camera and flash a press pass from your local law enforcement. A camera is very effective in keeping people on their toes. For experience, take some of your pictures to the media and find out if they will use them. At this point don't worry about getting paid, just try to establish some credibility. There's that word again.

Parades   Not too much to say about this, because we only used it a couple of times to show support for a person who was going to be fired by a disliked politician we had in our community. For this parade we used the Girl Scouts, Boy Scouts, youth groups, and some adults. We made our point and put a stop to this certain politician's BS. Use your imagination. A parade is effective but takes time to organize.

Picket   We on several occasions used pickets to get the attention of public officials when they were not responsive to the needs of the public—or should I say when their heads became a little too big for their hats. After having people stand outside of their office's front entrance for several days, they usually decided that it would be more politically expedient (if it is an elected official) if they would discuss the matter. If this happens to a department head, elected officials usually tell them to solve the problem and get the people off the streets. Signs with the right wording can be very nasty and effective, and people don't forget what is on those signs. Make sure that you write in big, bold letters and use black letters on a white background with a red border. Keep the verbiage to a minimum or people driving by can't read it.

Protest   When you want to get a little more aggressive, have people make noise, holler, and carry picket signs with nasty slogans. If you are angry, act like it; but have someone in charge who can keep it under control and know when enough is enough. With most of these activities, you shouldn't need a permit from the Police Department, but check it out ahead of time to avoid a hassle, and stay on public sidewalks.

Pamphleteering   This book has an entire chapter on pamphleteering, so I'm not going to spend too much time on it here. If done properly it can be as effective as newspapering. Make sure that whatever you write is accurate. Don't print it until several people have read it. I'm not talking about spelling and grammar, even though these are important. I'm talking about content accuracy. Distribute the pamphlets in places that will get the most results. Once you start on an issue, continue pounding on it until you win.

"CAUSES OF CORRUPT GOVERNMENT"

Excerpt from a speech by Clarence Manion,
Dean of Notre Dame Law School, 1952

A precision tool designed for one purpose will be entirely ineffective—may even be destroyed—in an attempt to use it for another purpose.

The American people, who know so much about tools and the use of tools, have completely lost sight of the purpose, object, and use of the tool of government.

Government is not now regarded merely as an instrument to restrain men from injuring one another, but as a sort of all-pupose, around-the-clock tool to make men happy and secure from the cradle to the grave.

CHAPTER 47

Letters to the Editor

WRITING LETTERS to the editor is a very effective undertaking for wanna-be activists. It's easy, and it is a way of getting your feet wet without drowning on your first time out (maybe). Letters to the editor in most newspapers is probably one of the best-read sections of the paper, because people want to know what other people are thinking or what stupid statement some knucklehead is spouting off about. Remember, if you decide to write a letter, don't go off half-cocked. Write your letter and read it every day for the next three or four days. Ask someone who you think will give you an honest evaluation to read and give an opinion of what you have written.

A man was talking to his best friend who wanted to go to work for him as a proofreader at his newspaper. He asked him, "Do you realize how important the job of proofreading is?" His friend replied, "Yes I do; whenever there is an error made, I take the blame and never say a word."

EVERYONE IS BIASED

This book or any book that I write will have a slant, slope, or twist. Well, let's be truthful. It will be biased toward the conservative point of view and with no apologies. So it will be with most anything you write. There is nothing wrong with writing your biased letters, as long as you realize they are biased. If you really want to cover your butt, include in your letter a statement stating that you are biased. If you admit you are biased, it will show that you're intelligent enough to know it and will make it more difficult for someone to attack you. After all, you do have a right to your biased opinions. Remember, for every letter you send, there will be some bleeding-heart, lefty liberal waiting to attack you with some stupid, utopian, daydreaming, no-logic, nonsense response. It will make no sense but sound wonderful. And since a majority of the population is liberal (according to the way they vote anyway), a healthy number of the newspaper readers probably will be left of center and tend to agree with their lefty liberal friends who attack you. You have been warned. Remember, it is very difficult to rebut no-logic daydreams, and you can't tell people they can't dream. How can you win a debate if you're arguing with someone who is discussing their subjective beliefs? You can't. Arguing liberal, socialist philosophy is similar to carrying on a useless debate with someone about religion. All religions think they are right, and all liberal, socialist-thinking people believe they have the solutions to social problems (socialism).

WATCH YOUR FLANK

More often than not, the attack will come from some over-degreed (you noticed that I didn't say over-educated), socialist-indoctrinated, college grad journalist working for your local newspaper. Don't leave yourself open for attack. Think before you act. Letter writing is an easy thing to do, but remember there are liabilities attached. Number one, anything that you put in writing can for years come back to slap you in the face. You go off half-cocked, write letters containing information you know nothing about, and five years later up pops your stupid old letters. If you are a group trying to accomplish a project and one of your members writes one of those stupid letters, it will discredit the entire group. Think, think, think. As soon as you become an activist, other alert activists from the opposing camps will be keeping their eyes on you and building a file of your stupid actions, just as you should be doing to them.

FIND A MENTOR

If you want to become an activist, find yourself a mentor, someone who has been around for awhile and has a few battle scars. Believe me, if there are any old timers in your area, they will jump at the chance to have volunteers to help in some of their battles. The best part of this is that you will be able to take advantage of their experience and save yourself a lot of hard knocks, wasted energy, and time.

How People Acquire Information		
Method:	Inspiration and Pondering	Reason and Logic	Osmosis and Testimony
Incidence in Population:	Very Rare	2–5%	95+%

John Stuart Mill was talking about this process when he said a new idea goes through three phases: "Ridicule, Argument, and Adoption." Victor Hugo talked about the third phase when he wrote, "An idea whose time . . ."

Where do people who don't read get their ideas??? They get them from people who do read. They acquire their ideas through testimony and osmosis. All (all??) we need to do is reach that 2–5% who think, write, speak, teach, preach, and persuade. They will popularize the idea for us. They know how to reach the masses. That is their job, not ours.

Is writing a solution? Mabye not. Depends who reads it; depends on what they do with it after they read it.

You can accomplish as much or more as an activist as you can by being elected to office.

CHAPTER 48

Free Born John Story

THE STORY of Free Born John is very fascinating, and it is a true story. One of our main P-Words, Pamphleteering, is what this story is all about. Our Founding Fathers were aware of Free Born John's deeds, and his deeds were instrumental in the framing of our Bill of Rights.

Free Born John (John Lilburn) was born in 1614 in Greenwich, England. He left school at the age of fifteen to work as an apprentice in the woolen trade in London. At the age of twenty-two, John read Dr. Bastwick's book, *Letany*, which had been illegally published. Dr. Bastwick had not obtained a license to publish; consequently, he was sentenced to jail but continued to write articles that were critical of the state church. For this his ears were mutilated, he spent time in the pillory in the public square, and he was sentenced to life in prison. Off your knees, and on your feet. Let's make sure we don't go back to those days.

BEATEN AND JAILED

Dr. Bastwick inspired Free Born John to write, so John moved to Holland where he was free to publish literature deemed illegal in

England. In 1636 Free Born John returned to London, at which time an informant turned him in for importing books to England. John refused to answer questions at his inquisition, so he was sent back to prison. Time after time the court tried to get him to admit to crimes against the state, but he refused to talk. He was fined, whipped, and placed in a pillory. They were going to cut off his ears, but because of public outcry his ears were spared. As he hung in the pillory with over 500 gashes in his back from the whipping he had received, swollen and bleeding, he talked to the crowd who had come to scorn him. When he refused to shut up, he was gagged. When he was released, the crowd who had come to scorn him became his supporters. He became a martyr. John not only spoke and wrote with conviction, he lived his convictions.

CHAINED HAND AND FOOT

When the whipping and the pillory failed to change John, for four months he was chained hand and foot. In spite of poor health, he survived his torture. He spent another three-and-a-half years in prison without a trial and still managed to continue his pamphleteering. You can thank Free Born John for the cruel and unusual punishment provision in our Bill of Rights.

WINS ONE

John was inducted into the King's army but during those years refused to take their oath because it was against his beliefs. John returned to London where he continued his pamphleteering. He was in and out of courts, refusing to submit to their demands and standing on the Magna Carta (1215), demanding his rights. (You should read this document and its history.) In October 1649 and in court again, the pamphleteer was in jeopardy of losing his life. He argued his case, discussed jury nullification and the burden of proof issue, demanded a public trial in an open court, and challenged the jurisdiction of the court. In essence, he put the government on trial. For one of the first times in his life he was found not guilty.

So what's the moral of this story? Well, if the point of the story was lost in the maze of problems of Free Born John, let me clarify it for you. I would say that this story illustrates that one person can make a difference, if that person has tenacity and conviction. It tells you that if you truly believe that you are right, don't let anyone stop you from making your point. It illustrates the effectiveness and powerfulness of the written word, and how pamphleteering can rattle the powers that be. The powers that be know that pamphleteering is effective because it educates the public, and they know it is difficult to control educated people. Why do you think we have government-controlled schools in this country? Do you think it might be to keep us po' fo'ks under control?

SOCIALIST AGENDA

If you have read the *Wee Wee* book, you know about Upton Sinclair (Chapter 15), who was the godfather of socialism in America. He and a group of his socialist followers infiltrated the universities with the socialist doctrine. I am not going to go into the entire story again, so if you have not read the book you must get a copy. But my point here is they did a good job, because now many of the people who go through the government school system end up with liberal, socialist tendencies. The college-educated bureaucrats and politicians, who lean to the liberal socialist left, are a majority, and they push their agenda on the unsuspecting public. Be alert and pay attention to what is going on. Upton Sinclair and other socialists are also very dedicated to their philosophical beliefs. Don't forget this. Your ultimate long-term goal as a patriot has to be to fight socialism. Most everything that is wrong with America today is caused by the liberal, socialist philo-sophical beliefs of the past and present socialist-thinking leaders of this country. How do you change this? You work hard at exposing who they are and how they think. You work extra hard at getting them out of office and preventing others from being re-elected. You do this at a local level where you can be effective.

A socialist was talking to a wealthy banker and told him it was not fair for him to have so much money when there were so many millions of people with practically nothing. He told him there should be a more equitable way to distribute the wealth. The wealthy banker called in his secretary and asked her to look up the world population. When she returned and gave him the figure, he made a few simple calculations, then told his secretary to make out a check for sixteen cents. "This," said the banker, "is your share of my wealth if I were to divide it equally among all the people in the world."

What makes today unbelievable is not the noise of bad people—but the silence of good people.

Silence is the virtue of fools.

—Francis Bacon

CHAPTER 49

Pamphleteering

How do you become a Pamphleteer? Well, in this day and age with computers and copy machines, it certainly is much easier than in the times of Free Born John. And there is almost no risk of going to jail for what you say. Keep in mind there are libel laws on the books, which protect people from printed untrue and defamatory statements. Libel is committed through writing, print, pictures, or signs. You have heard of the term "slander." This is defamation of a person's reputation through the spoken word. Remember, if you libel someone in writing, it is obviously much easier to prove than if it is spoken. You have to use good judgment if you decide to write an article about someone. I am not even going to try to give you any legal advice. After writing an article about someone, ask yourself if you would be angry if the article were about you. Would you want to go to an attorney and sue the person who wrote it?

PRIVATE CITIZENS OFF LIMITS

More good advice is not to write about private citizens. If you feel that a private citizen has done something which is contrary to the public good, and law enforcement will do nothing about it, proceed to attack law enforcement's lack of attention, or write an article discussing your elected officials' lack of interest. Make sure those in government who are in charge of keeping the peace do their job. If government wants to have their nose in everyone's business, make them enforce the law. Keep the following in mind about a public person: a public person is someone who is the public eye, someone who, by their own deeds, has made himself very visible in the community and is practicing activism, as you might be after reading this book. If a person has made himself a public person, he then has left himself open for scrutiny and criticism. If you get out front and kick some butt, be ready to get your butt kicked by another activist from the opposing camp. This is what it is all about. The object is to end up on top. This is why I stress over and over to be prepared and to know what you are talking about before putting your thoughts in writing, because it can come back to bite you in the ass.

BEAT UP GOVERNMENT

You usually can beat up government for not doing their job, without repercussions. As a matter of fact, the chief hazard of the profession of politics and working for government is that one is at all times open for public scrutiny. It is the public's right and your duty to keep a vigilant eye on government at all times. Excluding personnel records of the employees, you have a right to look at most of the records of government: processed lawsuits (once they are filed in court, they are then public record), offers on land, other purchases, etc., etc.

I have watched with great interest over the years the actions of angry people when they first get enthused about fighting government. When they go to a public meeting and speak, or when they write their first few articles or letters to the editor, they are very aggressive (as was I). If you don't learn anything else from this book, learn to stay calm and to go about your battle in an organized manner. After a period of time of fighting battles, most people I have observed go about their business in a more professional manner. Have you ever watched two attorneys battle in the courtroom and later go have a cup of coffee together and laugh and joke about their courtroom battle? You might as well have the same attitude, because if you don't, you will drive yourself nuts. You must expect that you are not going to win every battle that you fight. More about picking the winning battles in another chapter.

NO ONE CARES, SHE SAID! OH YEAH!

As in pamphleteering, think about your objective and plan how to reach the goal. Let's take a very simple example. While we were publishing the paper, an elderly lady called one day and told me she lived on a busy road and three or four of her cars had been demolished in her own driveway over the last ten years. She had called the Department of Transportation and asked them to look into fixing the corner so cars would not end up in her front yard. No one listened.

NOW COMES THE NEWSPAPER

We entered the scene and I asked this lady first to put in writing and in chronological order all documentation that would verify her story. I noticed over the years that if I asked people to document their story in writing, they were less likely to exaggerate, and the details of their story were more complete. It also made it much easier to investigate. In this case she had some pictures of her wrecked cars and some old newspaper articles and written statements from people who were aware of the road hazard.

GET IT STRAIGHT

If you are going to write articles and put them in print, know what you are talking about. In the fifteen years of publishing the newspaper, we had to publish about five minor retractions, which is incredible considering the type of stories we wrote week after week. Printing retractions in a newspaper is required when you don't get your facts straight. To have had to print only five retractions in fifteen years is a good indicator of how well we did our homework. The only difference between pamphleteering and newspapering is that a newspaper is usually printed every week, while pamphleteering is done sporadically.

I'm getting off the subject of the lady. We wrote a couple of articles, calling to the attention of the public the number of wrecks that had occurred on the corner the lady was talking about. Calling attention to the problem makes it rather difficult for the agency in charge not to do something about it. In the two months that followed, there were two more accidents on the corner, and people were hurt. Bingo! The lady's story was accurate, and we now have a government agency that is showing no concern for public safety. Do you understand where this is going? The next article politely brought this to the attention of the public, at which time the public started sending letters to our paper. In order to be more persuasive, we sent to the road department these letters, along with our newspaper articles. The elected officials then read the story. How do we know this? Because we circled the story in red and made sure they received a copy. We now have the public incensed and raising hell with the elected officials. Elected officials are embarrassed by the inaction and lack of concern of the road department, so they say something to the road department and guess what? The road gets fixed.

We applied a little political pain both to the elected officials and the road department. You can accomplish the same goal with a printed pamphlet. If you put enough pamphlets in the right places, you can cause the bureaucracy to move. But you have to apply steady, persistent pressure in the right places. One of the keys to pamphleteering is not to tell anyone the size of your distribution. Just make sure you put out enough to keep them wondering. To accomplish your mission, put out the first pamphlet to test the reaction, and then adjust as you go to fit the mood of the people.

AGITATE, BUT DON'T LOSE SIGHT

The key in pamphleteering and in any kind of activism is to agitate, agitate, agitate. But of course agitate the right people. This point is explained in the next chapter.

Don't lose sight of your duty as a pamphleteer always to include some educational information about government. As you gain knowledge about government, pass it on to your readers, just as I am now doing. You don't lose anything by sharing your knowledge with other people; you gain by having better-educated people. In this case we all gain, because the more that people learn, the more difficult it will be for government to control educated people. People have turned to government for their needs for so long that they have to be re-educated and re-directed. Government is the problem, not the solution. Pamphleteering is a vehicle to change this.

SHOW THEM SOMETHING NEW

When is the last time you think the public in general has seen a city or county budget? I would venture to say that most citizens never have. I copied pages out of our city and county budget books and printed them in our newspaper. I then received calls from people who could not believe what they were seeing. As a matter of fact, go to your city and county government and request a copy of their budget books. There is usually no charge, if they have extras. If they have none, go to your library. If the library doesn't have them, go to your county or city auditor's office.

DON'T USE RADICAL LANGUAGE OR TERMS

When you write or speak in public, keep the language on a very conservative level. If you don't, you will lose your audience. For example, if you write, "Our City Councilman, John Doe Smith, is a communist, left-wing pig, who is destroying our city with his hitler-like attitude and socialist propaganda-preaching political machine. He is making little commies out of our young people." Even if this were somewhat true, you would lose me, because it is wild, non-thinking rhetoric.

BETTER LIKE THIS

The writer should say something to the effect that "Councilman John Doe Smith has on several occasions made statements to the effect that there are many good qualities in the communist philosophy that should be taught to our children in grade school. I have written to Councilman Smith and have asked him to explain in detail what it is that he thinks is so great about the communist and socialist philosophy and why he thinks it should be taught to our children in the public schools. Maybe there is something that we patriots are missing. If any of you reading this letter to the editor know what this wonderful something is, please pass it on to the rest of us dummies so we can be indoctrinated." Which of these two letters do you think would provoke more thought? THINK, THINK, THINK.

ANOTHER FORM OF PAMPHLETEERING: POSTERING

Postering is similar to pamphleteering, except that it is very short, to the point, and quickly gets across a message as someone walks or drives by. Posters are very effective if done correctly. The mind will retain a graphic image longer than a written-out pamphlet. I can still remember years ago seeing news clips of posters that had been hung on walls in communist Russia and China. Postering is a fast and easy project if you carefully pick the time of night to distribute. If you concentrate your efforts and saturate a certain area, you will get the attention of your intended target. The object is to get your message to as many people as is economically possible. What better way to do this than having hundreds of posters on both sides of a busy street one morning.

Mr. Slowee said, "I er ah er am going to tell you something that might er ah er ah surprise you. I er er think. . . ."

Ms. Quickie replied, "Well this is a surprise I never noticed before. How long have you been thinking?"

But what of the minority? As the *Supreme Court has ruled, "The very purpose of the Bill of Rights was to withdraw certain subjects from the vicissitudes of political controversy, to place them beyond the reach of majorities.* One's right to life, liberty, and property, to free speech, a free press, freedom of worship and assembly, and other fundamental rights may not be submitted to vote; they depend on the outcome of no election." [Emphasis added.]

CHAPTER 50

Agitate, Agitate, Agitate

THERE IS A BOOK titled *Dedication and Leadership,* written by Douglas Hyde, published by University of Notre Dame Press, which all activists and wanna-be activists should read. The author is an ex-communist, and the Catholics asked him to tell them why the Communists were so strong in certain areas and the Catholics were so weak, and why the Communists were so strong as leaders. This book was written in 1969 when the Communists were going strong. Don't let the fact that they went down the tubes distract you from the fact that for many years they did a super job selling the worthless, subjective, socialist, utopian daydream. Think about that for a moment, folks. The Communist party (and it is a political party) had an agenda of selling the world on the idea of socialism. Selling the idea is probably not the right term for it in their case; forcing socialism on the world would be a better way to put it. If you were paying attention during those tumultuous years, you would have noticed that the Communists at the height of their efforts were agitating all around the world. They had brush fires going in at least ten countries around the world. What do you think would have happened if they would have had a good idea to promote?

The communist-like hitler (I many times don't capitalize these names because I don't like to show any respect for them) went to the youth and trained them. Take a look around and pay attention to what the enviros are doing today. They are going into the schools teaching kids to be good little enviros. They are using kids in television commercials, etc., etc.. They have gone all over the country agitating, protesting, spiking trees, putting sand in the gas tanks of logging equipment, and violating other peoples' rights. What did they get in the process? They received press—good or bad, they received free press. In the process of getting free press, they were able to attract other enviros around the country and around the world with similar philosophy. Do you realize how much it would cost to run ads on national television to get the same amount of attention that the media gave to them for free? It would have cost them millions. They used the media, or one could say that the media used the radical enviros to further an agenda. Remember, the media is filled with liberal, social-thinking people who are ready at a moment's notice to promote any group with whom they agree.

Now if you are a conservative patriot and you think you are going to get the same free blitz from the media as have your liberal counterparts, think twice. If you get free publicity, it more than likely will be negative. The following is a statement I wrote and published in my newspaper:

BILATERAL PROBLEM

The conscious, subliminal, progressive manipulation of the opinions of the masses is an important element of society. Those who manipulate this mechanism constitute an invisible force that is a controlling power in our country.

In other words, the media with its hidden agendas is a powerful force in this country, and it became that way by spoon-feeding the masses only what it wants them to hear. Of course, in this day and age, it is more difficult for the media to control what is fed to the public because it is no longer controlled by three major networks. Computers, copy machines, and pamphleteers also make it more difficult.

SOLUTION: A TRILATERAL DILEMMA

1. To change society's habits and opinions, one must reach the masses. 2. To reach the masses, one needs the support of the media. 3. To get media support, one needs the support of the advertisers. 4. To influence the advertisers, you have to boycott. 5. To boycott, you need to reach the masses. 6. To reach the masses, you need the support of the media. 7. To get media support. . . .

OH, OH, THE KIWI BIRD

This dilemma is kind of like the story of the Kiwi bird, which flew in ever smaller and smaller circles until it flew up its own ass. The trilateral dilemma is a vicious cycle that can never be solved unless the media is willing to give the coverage that is needed to reach the numbers of people needed to make changes. And the way you make changes is through agitation, agitation, agitation.

How do you go about causing agitation and controversy in your community? Number one, you want to try to get the attention of your local media, so you get the press coverage that you need. You might be surprised. Some newspapers will give you space in the letters to the editor, which is one of the best read parts of most newspapers. But to get front page, they will have to be in agreement with you or think that they can make a fool out of you. And they will do that anytime they can. They will try to sensationalize on your efforts, to make you look bad. That's why you have to think out what it is you are going to do.

BLITZING THE HOMELESS

A good example of a man with an idea and media connections is the guy who was able to get the attention of the media to do a blitz on the homeless. This media blitz lasted for about five years as you probably remember. I saw a chart showing the number of homeless over the last fifty years, and it has not risen much more than a few percentages per capita. The politicians over the last fifty years also have not given much attention to the problem. Then came the media blitz, and within a few months all the liberal politicians who could fit on the bandwagon climbed aboard and claimed they and they alone had a solution to the homeless problem. When the media blitz died down, so did all the wind from the politicians. My point here is that when the public and the politicians are bombarded day after day with an idea or issue, the pressure from the public begins to mount. The public starts to moan and groan and then, as soon as they test which way the wind is blowing politically, the politicians climb on the bandwagon. Of course, determining what will be of benefit to them is their highest priority, anything that will help them get re-elected.

PLAY TO WIN

The politicians on your home town city council are just as eager to retain their positions as are those at the state and federal level. If you could get into the head of a small town politician and access his daydream department, you probably would see visions of his winning elections for higher office. If you are going to play the political game and you are going to play to win, you have to think. Try to understand how your elected officials think, so that you will know how to apply the most effective political pain to get the job done with the least amount of effort. More on this in the chapter on political pain. The point here is to find out what will cause pain to certain elected officials then through agitation cause the pain to happen.

COMMUNISM: You have two cows. The government takes both of them and gives you part of the milk.

SOCIALISM: You have two cows. The government takes one and gives it to your neighbor.

FASCISM: You have two cows. The government takes both cows and sells you the milk.

NAZISM: You have two cows. The government takes both of them and shoots you.

BUREAUCRACY: You have two cows. The government takes both of them, shoots one, milks the other, then pours the milk down the drain.

CAPITALISM: You have two cows. You sell one of them and buy a bull.

Chew on those for a while. . . .

City Council

County Supervisor

CHAPTER 51

Political Pain

THROUGHOUT THE BOOK we have made mention of political pain, but in this chapter we will try to be more specific. For example, while we were publishing our newspaper, I lowered myself below the line of good taste a few of times by calling to the attention of the public certain off duty charades of our local politicians. When you publish a newspaper it is amazing what people tell you. If you keep this information to yourself and only insinuate that you know something, it is surprising what can be accomplished. The incidents I am talking about in these cases were not violations of the law but rather details they would not like their friends, family, and the public to know. Make mental notes, dog ear the pages, and once in awhile go back to them and refresh your memory.

FIND THE DIRT

Always look for dirt around town and start a file on all your local elected officials. Keep track of the information, and it doesn't matter how trivial you think it is at the moment; you will be surprised at how it will all fit together down the road. I know I'm repeating myself but humor me; after reading this book, DON'T GO OFF HALF COCKED and find a battle to fight. Take the time to know and understand how the politics in your community work. You will be amazed when you discover the powers behind the throne. It could be someone in the community who owns a successful business and gives nice campaign contributions, or it could be someone of no means but who is politically astute.

FINANCIAL RECORDS OF POLITICIANS

The best way to check out a certain elected official is to go to the Elections Department and ask to look at the financial statements that all elected officials are required to file. You also should look at the list of contributors and the amounts they have contributed. You will learn a lot about your elected officials by doing this, and you will be able to identify their political friends. As you then watch the local meetings, you will begin to understand why things happen in a certain way. I am not saying that your elected officials will be doing anything dishonest, they just might be influenced by the friends they keep.

THE GOLDEN RULE

Making note of all these techniques will certainly make it easier for you to apply political pain to try to get the results you want. There is no law that says if you learn of a local person of means who has influence with a certain politician that you can't apply a little pressure and pain on that person in order to obtain a result. Remember the Golden Rule: The man with the gold usually makes the rules. I would hope that the readers of this book will use all of the information in this book with discretion and for the good of the people as set forth by the Constitution. Read the Constitution. Study it, study it, and then study it some more. Study the first ten amendments of the Constitution, but do not stop there. Know and understand both your state and federal constitutions. You must know the rules of the game if you are going to play.

GOVERNMENT EMPLOYEES' RESTRICTIONS

Don't forget, some government agencies also require government employees to disclose their financial holdings. The reason for this is to prevent government employees from taking advantage of their positions and obtaining information for financial gain.

A PERSONAL EXPERIENCE

Let me give you one of the best examples of a government employee abusing his position. This actually happened to me seventeen or eighteen years ago, and I'm still angry about it. There was a small parcel of land next to my house, and I decided to buy it just to have as a buffer. I went to the City Engineering Department and a city employee told me it was a nonbuildable lot because it was too small. So I thought, why buy it if no one can build on it? Well, guess what, folks? A few months later I saw a couple of people looking at the lot, and I informed them that the lot was too small to build on. An older gentleman told me that they had bought it and that it was a buildable lot because his son who worked for the city told him it was. Folks, let me tell you there was a battle. This happened not long after I had moved to this small town, and no one knew much about my activist tendencies from the past, but I can tell you they sure found out.

KICK THEIR ASSES

The end result was I couldn't do much about their building the house, but I made their life miserable during the building process by doing nothing more than insisting that the Building Department do their job by requiring their fellow employee to enforce all the building codes. At one point the builder had to tear off seven feet from the front of the house because he had built on the setback. By the time the builder was finished, he had filed bankruptcy. And his son who worked for the City had me to deal with for several years after I bought the newspaper. We watched every move he made and caught him pulling several borderline deals. Finally, the City passed an ordinance prohibiting city employees from being involved in any after hours work that had any connection to the work they did in their city jobs. Mission accomplished.

USE GOOD JUDGMENT

This was about the only time I used my paper to fight a personal battle. As I have told you, it is better to fight your personal battles behind the scenes and other battles publicly. Use good judgment in using the power of the pen and press.

A government employee worked all morning digging a hole. His boss came by and said to fill it back up. So he filled it back up with the dirt, but he had a small pile of dirt left that would not fit back into the hole. When his boss came back later, he asked him what he should do. His boss thought for awhile and then told him to dig the hole deeper.

A Tax Foundation Study found that out of an 8-hour work day, Americans work 2 hours and 49 minutes to pay federal, state and local taxes. The rest goes like this:

HOUSEHOLD COSTS .... 1 hr. 23 min.
FOOD & DRINK .... 57 min.
HEALTH CARE .... 46 min.
TRANSPORTATION .... 38 min.
RECREATION .... 24 min.
CLOTHING .... 23 min.
MISCELLANEOUS .... 21 min.
SAVINGS .... 19 min.

—The American Way Features, 1990

The Constitution

In THIS CHAPTER we are going to look at the first ten amendments, THE BILL OF RIGHTS, to try to learn how it relates to us peons at the local level. I am no constitutional authority, and I'm sure some of you are more knowledgeable about the Constitution than I am. If you think you know it all, I guess you can skip this chapter.

In addition to the first ten amendments, the Preamble to the Constitution is another area that should be discussed. It says:

We, the people of the United States, in order to form a more perfect union, establish justice, insure domestic tranquillity, provide for a common defense, *promote the general welfare*, and secure the blessings of liberty to ourselves and our posterity, do ordain and establish this Constitution for the United States of America.

PLEASE READ IT MORE THAN ONCE

PROMOTE OR PROVIDE?

I emphasized *"promote the general welfare"* for a good reason. It does not say PROVIDE for the general welfare. There is a great difference between promoting and providing. When government promotes the general welfare, it makes people responsible; but when government provides the general welfare, it makes people irresponsible.

DEFINITION OF PREAMBLE

I also want you to know that there has been a Supreme Court ruling stating that the Preamble to the Constitution is not a part of the document. It is just what it says it is, and that is the "Preamble." A "Preamble" is an interpretation of any ambiguities within the statute to which it is prefixed. (*Griffith v. New Mexico Public Service Comm.*, 86 N.M.113,520 p.2d 269.271.)

WHAT'S THE POINT

I made this point for a reason. Many of the liberals use this statement, "promoting the general welfare," to justify their demands for more social programs. It does not say "provide," it says "promote," and even if it said "provide," it is not part of the legal document. As you read through the U.S. Constitution, try to find any statements that give the United States government the authority to provide welfare for people.

I am not going to print all ten amendments, so if you don't have a copy of the United States Constitution, please get one. Also get a copy of your state constitution.

THE BEHEADED BILL OF RIGHTS

Now that we have discussed the preamble to the Constitution, let's talk about the Preamble to the Bill of Rights. Did you find this in your copy of the Constitution? It should be at the beginning of the Bill of Rights. Well, if you don't find it, don't be alarmed because it was removed in the 1930s. Gee, folks, wasn't that about the time of the great socialist experimenter, F.D.R., and his New Deal drive to turn our Representative Republic into a Socialist Welfare State? If the

Preamble to the Constitution were removed, the entire interpretation would change. Do you think maybe that's why F.D.R. and his constitutional rapists removed the Preamble to the Bill of Rights? You read it and you decide.

THE ORIGINAL PREAMBLE TO THE BILL OF RIGHTS

"The conventions of a number of the States, having at the time of their adoption of the Constitution expressed a desire, in order to prevent misconstruction or abuse of its powers, that further declaratory and restrictive clauses should be added: And as extending the ground of public confidence in the Government, will best insure the beneficent ends of its institutions."

After reading the original preamble, do you think our Founding Fathers had a fairly good idea what would happen if government were not restricted? Do you think the Bill of Rights (the first ten amendments) have been distorted over the years? Do you think that government has over-stepped its originally intended authority?

AMENDMENT 1

As you read the Constitution, you will notice that it is in very plain, easy, understandable language. You will also notice that almost everything is written as restrictions for government, not for the people. Our Founding Fathers came to this country for freedom, and the only way to have freedom was to restrict government. It looks to me as if we the people have dropped the ball and allowed the tables to be turned on us. We the people are the restricted ones. You have to read *Did Big Brother Give You Permission to Go Wee Wee?*

The First Amendment restricts government from interfering with religion, free speech, the right of the people to peaceably assemble, and the right to petition government for a redress of grievance, meaning you as a citizen have the right to say what you want to say about your government. You can write articles in newspapers or be a pamphleteer and demand that government right the wrongs that it has committed.

Good luck in getting them to do this, but you do have the right to try. Have patience.

AMENDMENT 2

"The right to keep and bear arms shall not be infringed". Sounds rather simple doesn't it? What is the problem, and why are the gun controllers trying to take away guns? I guess they can't read. The Second Amendment does not say the right to keep and bear CERTAIN arms shall not be infringed, does it? So why are the gun grabbers being allowed to pass gun regulation, which very clearly seems to be in violation of the law of the land? Our Founding Fathers knew the dangers of an unarmed citizenry; but if you make any reference to the possibility of a conflict between the government and the people, you are considered a radical.

AMENDMENT 4

Read this amendment very closely, because this is the amendment that is being violated time after time by government agencies, from Animal Control to Law Enforcement and its enforcement of asset forfeiture.

AMENDMENT 5

This also is a very important amendment for you to understand. It is about due process of the law. Over the years publishing the newspaper, we were able to put a stop to some of the actions of government agencies by demanding that they abide by this law of the land. In one case, Animal Control was picking up animals without first having a hearing (no due process of law for the citizen). Keep your eyes open for these types of violations.

AMENDMENT 9

CERTAIN RIGHTS NOT DENIED TO THE PEOPLE

(Section 1) The enumeration in the Constitution, of certain rights, shall not be construed to deny or disparage others retained by the people.

This amendment needs a lot of thought. Read it and think about it. Believe or not, this is one of the most important amendments when it comes to your freedom but has been lost in the shuffle and almost never spoken of.

AMENDMENT 10

(Section 1) The powers not delegated to the United States by the Constitution, nor prohibited by it to the States, are reserved to the states respectively, or to the people.

This is another important amendment you don't hear discussed much.

AMENDMENT 14

I am throwing in the Fourteenth Amendment because it is vital to any activist.

This is another amendment dealing with due process of the law. Become well educated on this one. As you read this amendment, ask yourself what does "nor be deprived of life, liberty or property, without due process of law" mean to you? You have a right to your opinions on what this means to you.

Read and study both your state and federal constitutions. KNOW THE RULES and use them to keep your government in check.

LINCOLN said, "Study the Constitution!"

Let every American, every lover of liberty, every well-wisher to his posterity swear by the blood of the Revolution never to violate in the least particular the laws of the country, and never to tolerate their violation by others. As the patriots of '76 did to the support of the Declaration of Independence, so to the support of the Constitution and laws let every American pledge his life, his property, and his sacred honor. Let every man remember that to violate the law is to trample on the blood of his father, and to tear the charter of his own and his children's liberty. . . . Let it be taught in schools, in seminaries, and in colleges, let it be written in primers, in spelling books and in almanacs, let it be preached from the pulpit, proclaimed in legislative halls, and enforced in courts of justice. And, in short, let it become the political religion of the nation, and, in particular, a reverence for the Constitution.

—Abraham Lincoln

CHAPTER 53

Alone or With Someone

IF YOU ARE A LONER you can accomplish your objectives but you have to do all the work yourself. Sometimes this ain't all bad. Sometimes it seems to take more energy to keep a group together than it does to go do the project yourself. But there are times when one body at a public forum just don't get it. I have learned over the years that elected officials listen and pay attention to numbers. If you were an elected official and one lone person came before you at a public meeting with a complaint, would you pay as much attention to him as you would to a mob of 100 to 200 or more people? I use the term "mob" because that's what it is, mobocracy.

DEMOCRACY, MY PET PEEVE

When you read the *Wee Wee* book you will find that the term "democracy" is my pet peeve. Our form of government is a representative Republic. Read Article Four, Section Four, of the U.S. Constitution. It says every state in this union *SHALL* be guaranteed a

Republican form of government. Democracy is a form of government in which a majority vote of the people is the rule. We don't have this type of government, and we don't want it. An example of democracy is two foxes and a chicken voting on what's for dinner. The sad thing is that mobocracy does work at public meetings; therefore, use it to your advantage. Make sure that what you want done is not infringing on someone else's rights. Sometimes we look at issues only from our own point of view, so always ask yourself if you would like the same thing done to you. Don't forget that your point of view may be distorted by your angle of vision.

GET TOGETHER A GROUP

If you want to organize a group of people to fight a certain battle, start by identifying other people who are emotional about the issue. For example, let's say the city is planning to raise the water rates, and a big percentage of retired people lives in mobile parks and retirement projects. What are you going to do first? I would say that you should get out your pencil and paper and do some exaggerating. Now don't get me wrong. I don't want you to lie. I want you to make the figures work in your favor so you can accomplish your mission of stopping the city from raising the rates. Do your homework. Get a copy of the budget of the city's water department and go over it with a fine tooth comb. Anything that you don't understand, ask the person in charge of the water department. Never talk to employees. Always talk to the people in charge unless you know some of the employees and promise to keep confidential any information that they give you. You must never, never divulge your sources of information, or they will dry up real fast. There are many employees who see waste but don't want to lose a good-paying government job by causing trouble. If you are going to be a watchdog of government operations, cultivate good sources. Many times employees came to me because their boss was a real knucklehead and they wanted to get him fired. I obliged and helped several get fired. Some just resigned.

MAKE YOUR FIGURES WORK FOR YOU

As I started to say, make your figures work for you. Instead of showing how much it is going to cost each resident per month for the increase in the water rate, multiply it out for a year. For a large number of residents in a mobile home park, multiply it times all the residents for the next five years. Agitate the retired people on fixed incomes and get them to rally around you at a public meeting. Provide transportation for people. It all evolves around thinking out your battle strategy. You should always look at these confrontations as war—you against them. Government is well-organized and schooled in the fine art of public debate and battle. Most government agencies belong to state and federal organizations that hold yearly conventions and seminars teaching their members how to co-opt people into complying. If you have a loosely organized group, they often will try to co-opt into voluntary compliance members of your group who they think will influence other members. You soon are standing all by yourself and don't know what happened to you.

LIKE PLAYING CHESS

As I'm writing this, I continue to tell myself that all this sounds too complicated and people are going to be afraid to even get started. Don't let this happen to you. The object here is to make you aware of some of the pitfalls. It all boils down to thinking ahead of yourself. It's sort of like playing chess. You have to think three or four moves ahead of yourself. By being aware of some of these things, you will have less chance of being knocked off your feet by the unexpected, and a greater chance of anticipating the plays. Don't get discouraged.

BODY POWER

The power of numbers will usually work for you, because the elected officials see votes. They are smart enough to know that for every person who shows up at a public meeting, each has ten friends who think the way he does. Not being re-elected is the ultimate political pain.

The secret of power is the knowledge that you have more than the other guy. Figure that one.

ARTICLE IV.
THE STATES AND THE FEDERAL GOVERNMENT
Section 4. Protections of States Guaranteed

Republican Form of Government
The United States shall guarantee to every State in this Union a *republican* form of government, and shall protect each of them against invasion; and on application of the Legislature, or of the Executive (when the Legislature cannot be convened) against domestic violence.

•

DEMOCRACY is Lucifer's Most Effective and Most Subtle Form of Imitation Government

•

I pledge allegiance to the flag and to the DEMOCRACY for which it stands . . .

CHAPTER 54

Picking Your Battles to Build Credibility

OF ALL THE ADVICE I can give you, this has to be the most important. Pick and choose your battles. Win, win, win, and build credibility.

PEOPLE LOVE A WINNER

Have you ever noticed how people like to be associated with a winner and will do anything to stay clear of a loser? Someone wins the lottery, and he has so many new friends he doesn't know what to do with them. An athlete wins the elusive gold medal, and presto, all the major companies want him to endorse their products. It makes no difference whether you live in a small town or a big city, people want to associate with a winner. This is why it is so important to pick battles you can win.

NO-LOSE BATTLES

There are some no-lose battles wherein no matter what the outcome you still maintain your respectability. If there is a real scoundrel of a politician who is not well-liked, and you expose something he does and try to make him rectify his wrong but can't accomplish the mission, most people will be grateful that you had the fortitude to try. If your local government is trying to pass a new tax, and you fight and lose, you are still the good guy on the block for trying. You have to know, no matter what you do or what battle you fight, you are going to make some friends and you are going to make some political enemies. The object is not to anger the very people you are going to need on your side when the important battles come along.

BEHIND THE SCENES

Again, don't get me wrong and think you should only get in a battle in which you are assured of winning. Just cut your losses and build credibility. You can play the game just like the big boys if you are smart and do all your work behind the scenes. You can use the good tool the telephone and start working and agitating behind the scenes. Start rumors flying that will cause your opposition to come out of the woodwork and defend themselves. Put your opponent on the defensive and make him keep defending himself. Root out the behind-the-scenes players in the opposition camp.

Many people never work out in the open. They spend all their time in little private meetings scheming and plotting. There was a city council member in our city who rarely spoke at council meetings except to say, "I second the motion." But behind the scenes he was relentless in his never-ending quest to control and manipulate what happened in the city. In this case we tapped into his grapevine and knew what he was up to most of the time. The grapevine I just mentioned exists in most communities, and you should know how it works and try to get yourself on it. The reason is not only to know what the opposition is doing but to pass around some information you want passed around town on the QT. If you give information to someone in the opposition's camp and make sure they understand they are not to tell anyone, I can guarantee that within an hour or so it will be all over town or at least in the hands of the wrong people—or the right people if you planned it correctly. Use your own imagination on some of these ideas. This book is not meant to be a step-by-step guide; it is meant to make you think and to get the creative juices flowing.

MUST WIN

The battles we fought with our newspaper were not life and death battles, but they were battles that made a difference in our community. In the fourteen years we owned the newspaper, we fought so many battles that I can't begin to recall all of them. I would say the biggest percentage of the battles were fought behind the scenes. But we had the power of the pen and the newspaper for backup when we needed it, and the people in government knew that we knew how to use them. This is why it is so important to win battles and build credibility. Once people in government or anyone else knows that you know how to win, they think twice before starting a confrontation with you, because they know you will stick to it until you prevail. This gives you a little bargaining power.

GIVE THEM FIRST OPTION

First you ask government to fix a problem, and if they don't do anything about it you can mention that it surely would make a good story, and you would love to print an article or a letter to the editor. If the battle is with a bureaucrat, he won't want his bosses to read about it in the paper. If it is printed in the paper it makes the elected officials and/or their superiors look bad, so this will force the elected officials to have a conference with the department head, and if you are right about what you are complaining about, it will probably be fixed. If not, the battle then begins, and you had better be right. Have your ducks in place and go for it.

If you perfect your pamphleteering, you can have almost as much effect as someone with a small newspaper. Pamphleteering is great because you don't have to put one out week after week, which means you have less work day after day. Take my word for it, pamphleteering is the weapon of choice among those in the know.

PAMPHLETEERING NATIONWIDE

Someone I once helped is a good example of a very effective pamphleteer. This person saw a real problem. I ran some articles for him and told him he should be a pamphleteer. I gave him a copy of the story about Free Born John. This motivated him. I then gave him a few tips, and he was off and running. He made contacts all over the United States and motivated other people to run copies of his pamphlets and asked them to hand them out for him. He sent specially-designed pamphlets to target different organizations all over the country. He figured out in what way each was affected by the problem and then used his creative ability to embellish the story and gore their ox to create a desire for them to make and hand out pamphlets to protect their own self-interests. Self-interest is a great motivator; use it! He always researched his subject and studied to make sure he did not tarnish his reputation. Through his efforts he educated thousands of people. His pamphlets were good enough that newspapers were reprinting them all over the country. He did a great job, and we can thank Free Born John for that.

COPY CATS

If or when you start pamphleteering, encourage people who receive a copy to copy it and fax it to everyone they know. As a matter of fact, you should print "copyrighted" at the bottom of your pamphlet. You do this by simply printing the copyright symbol, which is a circle with the letter c inside: ©, or you can write out the word "copyright" and the date. BUT PAY ATTENTION! After listing the copyright, you then can give people permission to reprint as long as it is reprinted in its entirety. This prevents people from picking bits and pieces of your writing and distorting it accidentally or on purpose to discredit you and your project. Don't think for one moment your opposition will not try to make you eat your own words if they can. And of course you will learn to do the same thing to them. This is why I tell you to read and re-read what you write. Then let an objective person look it over and give you an honest evaluation. The object here is damage control. Stop the damage from happening, so you later will not have to waste your time trying to explain your way out of some stupid statement you made without thinking it out.

A NEVER-ENDING BATTLE

If you're interested in a never-ending battle, try working on the welfare system in your county. Remember that most of the money and rules for welfare come from the state and federal government. But check out your county, and if you live in a bigger city check them out also. Counties and cities sometimes have a certain amount of their own money that is spent on give-away programs. Go to the Auditor Controller or the person who puts together the yearly budget book. They have to report where all the money goes. Be careful with that statement. They are *supposed* to report all the money, but sometimes it is reported in areas in which you would never think to look. In other words, it can be lumped into an unrelated category—usually legally. So look carefully and ask many questions. You will be surprised what you will uncover if you ask enough questions. I have discovered over the years that most people in government will answer but will not volunteer. The welfare issue is a never-ending battle and will keep you busy until the socialist agenda is snuffed.

MULTIPLE BATTLES

You'll quickly realize you will need more than one battle going at a time because most of them can't be rushed. If you maintain a file on each project and continue to add information, you will have a good case to present. The welfare issue is one of those no-lose battles that can be an ongoing fight, even if you are doing nothing more than continually exposing what it is they are doing. Take my word for it on this one. There are very few people who will come forward publicly to support the welfare system, so no matter what you expose through letters to the editor or pamphleteering, the public in general will be on your side and will look forward to more information. Be accurate, that's all I ask. If you're accurate, I'm pretty sure you won't get yourself in trouble, and you'll have fun in the process.

A merchant one day gave me a welfare voucher (this is a slip of paper welfare gives to a welfare recipient to buy goods at the store). The merchant sold clothing and sporting goods. The merchant is required to print on the voucher what is purchased. This particular voucher showed that the welfare recipient had purchased a .22 caliber rifle, some ammunition, and fishing gear. When I printed this voucher in the newspaper, people were very irate, and without much of a battle the end result was reform in the voucher system. The new voucher read "for necessities only." End of that battle, one for our side. You never know from where your leads will come. All you have to do is show that you are a person who is willing to expose the "wrongs," and that you will not divulge your sources. Build that credibility.

PRICE-FIXING

Here's another example. One day someone telephoned me, upset because the manager of the county fair told the exhibitors they all had to charge the same price for soft drinks. I checked it out, and sure enough this was true. Off the top of my head I told the manager this was price-fixing, and it restricted the rights of the exhibitors to competitive, free market pricing. The manager was being stubborn, so I went to one of the county supervisors and told him about the problem. What I did next is something you must remember when you need a legal opinion on government issues. I asked the supervisor to get an opinion from the County Counsel, which is the attorney for the Board of Supervisors. The legal opinion was that the fair manager should cease and desist. Mission accomplished, no legal fees. The County Counsel is not a legal service for the public. Their function is to keep the elected officials out of trouble. So if you see a problem that looks like it could cause heartburn for the taxpayers, ask one of your elected representatives to get a legal opinion from their legal beagles. At the city level, the legal counsel is called the City Attorney. At the state and federal level, they are called the Legislative Counsel.

ODD & EVEN COURT FIGHT

In the *Wee Wee* book I wrote about a great battle we won against the municipal court judges who set up an illegal traffic ticket operation. We interpreted the law one way, and they interpreted it another way. I asked our state assemblyman to get a Legislative Counsel opinion, and their opinion agreed with what we said. This had enough influence on the three appellate court judges that we won, and the municipal court judges had to stop the illegal odd and even ticket issuing. We don't know yet for sure, but this case might be published in the law books (*Metzger v. The People of California*). This battle lasted about three years. With the help of a patriot lawyer, we filed all of our own papers and it reached all the way to the local appellate court. We argued our own case.

YOU AGAINST THE WORLD

Some battles that you win really make you feel good, because while you are fighting them you sometimes feel it's you against the whole world. As bad as the legal system is, it does work. Remember, folks, no matter how much wrong I think there is with our government, it is still the best in the world. That's scary. But just because I say it is still the best does not mean any of us can sit on our laurels hoping it is going to straighten itself out. It should be rather evident to anyone who is even half awake that our Founding Fathers would roll over in their graves if they saw our government today. The title of my first book, *Did Big Brother Give You Permission to Go Wee Wee?*, says it all. There is nothing we can do that is not touched directly or indirectly by regulation or taxation. This is sad, isn't it? Especially when you logically look at all the laws and regulation. Honest people don't need all these laws to carry on their daily lives, and crooks don't obey them. So what's the point? Could it be to control honest people?

As the Senator rose at a town meeting, he said, "I rise to a point of information." A bystander shouted out, "I'm glad to hear it, because you need it."

WATCH IT

Watch your thoughts, they become words.
Watch your words, they become actions.
Watch your actions, they become habits.
Watch your habits, they become character.
Watch your character, it becomes your destiny.

—Frank Outlaw

CHAPTER 55

Friendly Persuasion

BEFORE YOU DO ANYTHING aggressive, always try diplomacy. It never hurts to try to solve problems diplomatically rather than by conflict. I should say, you should always try to solve problems peacefully. I have discovered over the years that people in government will listen but usually can't do anything to solve problems you take to them, because they are required to follow the rules, so it is a matter of trying to get the people who make the laws to make the changes. I also should qualify this statement by telling you that people in government were willing to listen to me after I had shown that I would not give up and had won battles to prove myself. It's kind of like a boxer. Until he has proven himself by working his way up the ladder of contenders, he is not given a shot at the big boys.

LOOK FROM ANOTHER ANGLE

You always want to step back and put yourself in the position of the other party. Ask yourself how you would react if you were in the other person's shoes. If someone has a problem with you, and they come at you like a bull in a china cabinet, how would you react? And please don't go into a government office making statements like, "I pay your wages, you work for me," etc., etc. Ranting and raving, screaming and hollering will not solve anything. If you act like this you only discredit yourself, and if you have a group it discredits the entire group. I am fully aware of how easy it is to pull those stupid tricks because I have done it myself.

DON'T GET PISSED

When they first get involved in a struggle with government, many people are already at the point of exploding out of sheer frustration. It seems so simple—all the person behind the desk would have to do is make a very simple decision, and the problem would be solved. However, it doesn't usually work like this. Most of the time government is doing only what the rule book says it can do.

BORING GOVERNMENT JOBS

Studies have been done concerning government jobs and how boring most of them are. We are talking about the front desk jockeys and paper pushers, not the elected officials and the bureaucrats. Why are the jobs so boring? Well, it is no different than the story I wrote in the *Wee Wee* book about the man who gets up in the morning, reaches for his daily rule book, and then proceeds to follow it all day long, day after day, week after week, year after year. This is what it is like working a government job. They have to do everything by the book, day after day, week after week, and year after year. I could never understand why so many people in government request medical stress leaves or stress retirement. I interviewed a few government employees, and they all admitted they had good paying jobs, but after the newness wore off it was boring, boring, boring.

DON'T GET ME WRONG

Now don't get me wrong. I'm not telling you this because I want you to feel sorry for government employees. I just want you to think and understand that there are two sides to every story. Look at both sides before you go kicking and screaming after some government employee. My argument against any government employee who has been rude to me is, if you don't like your job, get another one. I guarantee you there is a line two blocks long waiting to get your job. I have little tolerance for rude and discourteous government employees, as you would know if you had been reading my writing over the years. The real point here is, you can benefit from my mistakes and solve problems faster if you go through the proper channels and use a little diplomacy.

Actually, there are usually three sides to every story: her side, his side, and the truth somewhere in between.

FIRST BIG ONE

One of my first big battles with government was over arrogant, rude employees, and one of my last battles before selling the newspaper was about arrogant, rude employees. In the last battle I took my own advice and went directly to the employee's boss, who refused to do anything about the problem. So I ended up talking to the Personnel Department, who then solved the problem by sending the two employees through a public relations course. Mission accomplished, and I never got any heartburn. As a matter of fact, during the almost fifteen years publishing the newspaper and fighting battles, I almost never allowed myself to get upset. If you show anger or get angry, you are the loser. Control yourself. After having been coached and told to have their speeches written out, I have seen people get up in public meetings and make complete asses of themselves. I don't want you to discredit yourself, because it is difficult to undo those types of situations. Bad news travels twice as fast as good news.

PUBLIC MEETINGS

Since we are on the subject of public meetings, there are a couple of ideas I should bring up. Elected officials are supposed to make their decisions based on information they receive at a public meeting. The object is to give the public the same opportunity to hear the same arguments for and against that the elected officials are hearing. I mention the Brown Act in another chapter of the book, and this is to insure that public issues are discussed in public. But I can tell you from years of experience, most elected officials have a fairly good idea how they are going to vote before they go into a public hearing. It would be naive for you think any differently.

BEWARE

So with this in mind, you can also play the game by contacting the elected officials prior to the meeting and stating your case. You have to be careful not to violate the Brown Act in California by talking to more than two elected officials on a body of five. If you feel the need to talk to more than two, you do this by having other people talk to some of them. You can also talk to the bureaucrats who are usually asked to give their recommendations to the elected officials in the public meeting. You have to be careful if you are asking the public body to make a decision that would benefit you. The object of this book is not to teach you how to use the system to benefit yourself.

One bureaucrat to another: "So we made a blunder! Don't just stand there—label it 'Top Secret' and file it."

CHAPTER 56

Newspapering

AFTER YOU HAVE done some pamphleteering, gotten your feet wet in the political battleground, and discovered that if you are accurate in what you print, no one is going to come and haul you off, then you should be about ready to try newspapering. As we discuss starting a newspaper, we are going to be talking about starting one with very little money. I believe the best way is to start slowly and work your way up, instead of starting off big and working your way down. Even if you can afford to invest several thousand dollars in a newspaper to begin with, why not first test the water? Find out if the public is going to accept your style of writing. It also will give you an opportunity to get a feel for what your future advertisers think.

BULLDOBER

Make up your mind right from the get-go, you are going to be a watchdog newspaper of the bulldog type. I always described my newspaper as a cross between a Pitbull and a Doberman. The fighting instincts of the Doberman are to run in and rip and tear, and the Pitbull never lets go. Be a Bulldober.

LOW BUDGET NEWSPAPERING

I helped several people start up newspapers. If you will listen to me, you can get started in the newspaper business for very little cost. The best size paper to start with is what is called a bobtail tab (a tabloid), which is the size of the *National Enquirer*. It is a good size because it can be put in a file folder or a brief case, it's easy to read in a restaurant, and it costs less to print. Please keep in mind, what I'm going to tell you now are the very basics of the operation. It's like everything else I'm telling you about in this book. It's more compli- cated than what I have the time and space to explain in detail. But if you pay attention, you should be able to feel your way through the process without getting into too much trouble. The paper we published for fifteen years was a tab and approved by the court (adjudicated) to publish legal notices. We had to publish every week by law. You don't need this, and it takes a year of continuous publishing to qualify for adjudication.

FLEXIBILITY

To begin with, you want a paper that is flexible enough you can publish when you want to, at least until you get a feel for what you are doing. I always suggest putting out a once-a-month paper first. Putting out a paper every week is a chore, believe me.

COST

The cost to print a twenty-page tab is governed by the quantity of papers you print. The major cost of setup is placed on the first thousand papers. If you take the printer camera-ready copy, your cost should be $200.00 to $300.00 for the first 1,000 papers. You then pay thereafter a cost of somewhere in the ballpark of $40.00 to $60.00 per thousand papers. Again, the price per thousand fluctuates depending on the total quantity of papers you are printing. It also depends on what year you read this book. I can just see someone picking up a copy of this book fifty years from now and saying, "Newspaper! What's that?" The best thing to do is find a newspaper printer, tell them you are a novice, and ask them if they will guide you through the process on the first couple of runs. When we bought the newspaper, we didn't even know what a web press was. If you don't know what it is, think back to some movie showing a press with paper going from one roller to another and newspapers flying out of the end of a printing press. That's a web press.

DON'T RUSH

You want to be able to give yourself enough time on the first issues so you don't feel pressed to go to press on a certain day. Of course, you have to work out a press time with the printer. Once you set a date and time, you had better be there, or you won't get your paper as planned. If I were you, I would pay close attention to what I'm now going to tell you. Don't try to print current events. It won't be news if it is not printed on time. You don't need this to deal with, and most of those happenings are not that important in the scheme of things.

There are two sayings and they go like this: Haste makes waste, and he who waits has lost. Are you real confused now?

STICK TO GOVERNMENT

I should clarify that last statement. If you are going to produce a newspaper to print stories about car wrecks, rainstorms, murder, rape, violence, and high school sports, you are reading the wrong book. On the other hand, if you want to be an activist and print government information, information the people need to know about, then keep on reading. There is more than likely a newspaper in your town that prints the garbage. What the people need is the truth about what government is doing to them.

YOUR CHOICE

Deciding what to put in your paper is obviously going to be up to you, at least until the readers start giving you feedback. I found over the years that the information most people wanted was political issues, activities of the elected officials in public meetings, new laws and new fees, etc., etc. To get this information you don't have to attend any meetings. All you have to do is make a request to receive, as a newspaper or citizen, the same information packet your city council or county supervisors receive for their public meetings.

GET THE PACKET

You will be amazed at the material in those packets, material which needs to be printed. If you are not printing a paper to try to win awards for appearance, the best thing to do is reprint actual documents. The readers like it because they can see you have not manipulated the material in any way. The highest priority to establish from the beginning is that you will always print the facts and let the readers make up their own minds. Don't be overly concerned about winning awards for journalism. As a matter of fact, whenever someone called me a journalist, I told them I considered it an insult. I was a newspaper publisher with one thing in mind—getting out information. People always told me the charm of our paper was its unusualness and straightforward, no-BS style. Now that was a compliment.

EDITORIALS ARE JUST THAT

When you write editorials you can exercise your rights of freedom of speech to the hilt, and you should. I hope you will use good judgment and kick the right people in the ass. It seemed the tougher and more critical I was, the more the readers liked it. When I got lazy and wrote mushy editorials, we received less mail. The harder I hit the bureaucrats and politicians, the more letters and phone calls we received. Make sure you know what you are talking about. Check, check, check your facts. If your story is going to anger quite a few people, double check your sources and question the opposition. A few potentially great stories fell apart because I was not told the truth by my source.

BE CAREFUL

If you print a story about a person in government and use their name, you had better be right. If you write articles about an agency or some government activity, you are cut a little slack if you're not right on target, but they will let you know about it.

INFO GALORE

People want to know about government activities and issues, and most newspapers don't keep them informed. You will find if you report these types of issues, you will never run out of material to print, and you don't have to run all over town looking for it; it comes to you.

SCRATCHING THE SURFACE

What I am printing here just scratches the surface of newspapering. It is one of the most interesting occupations or hobbies you will ever do. Be careful, it is very addicting. Aside from the fun and interesting aspects of newspapering, it is a necessity. Every community needs a minimum of two newspapers, both having opposing views; otherwise, what is the point?

FEEL IT OUT

In the chapter covering pamphleteering, we discussed some of the topics you should pamphleteer. The same ideas apply to newspapering. When you first get started with your newspaper, it is probably a good idea to print at least two issues. If you then feel good about them, and you have received some good feedback from the public, then approach some business people you know who hopefully are in agreement with your cause or views. Ask them if they will run a business card-sized ad in your paper. Over the years I found that even if business people didn't agree with everything I printed, they agreed it was good to have another opinion in the community. They will advertise because they know there is a group of people out there reading your paper, and most of them know that advertising is a part of doing business.

DON'T DO STUPID THINGS

If you are not doing stupid things such as writing derogatory articles about local businesses, you will probably be supported by the local businesses. Keep in mind people in business are the ones who are beat up the most by government through regulations. So, if you are writing the types of articles you should be writing and you are being a watchdog for the business community, they will appreciate what you are doing. Get the message? Having been in business for twenty years before I bought the newspaper, I already knew many of the concerns of the business community. If you aren't aware of the concerns, you should head out into the streets and find out what is being talked about. Keep yourself available to the public at all times. Don't wait to hear from them. Get out there and make it your business to know what they are thinking. In the chapter on picking your battles, I believe I mentioned how important it is to be out among the public and know what the public is thinking.

EASY ECONOMICS

Here's a quick economics lesson on pricing: If we take the figure I gave you earlier of about $250.00 to run the first 1,000 papers, you would have to sell ten ads at $25.00 each to pay for the 1,000 papers. If you run 5,000 papers, you pay $250.00 for the first 1,000, and you pay $50.00 for each of the other 4,000 papers. This equals $200.00. Add this together and you have a total of $450.00. If you run 5,000 papers, you can charge a little more per ad, because the ad is reaching more people. If someone paid $50.00 for an ad and it reached 5,000 homes, it only cost the advertiser ten cents per home. For this price, a business person couldn't even pay the postage on an envelope. Are you getting the idea?

DISTRIBUTION

If you have an activist group of ten people, each one of you can take 500 papers and distribute them to businesses, restaurants, or any place the local people frequent. You can target a specific area, maybe a residential area. Depending on what you have printed in the paper, you will want to saturate the area of concern. The object is to agitate, agitate, agitate. You agitate by educating the public on issues that are rarely brought to their attention. If you have a newspaper, it is your job to keep the public informed on government activities and issues, and hopefully if government is doing something they shouldn't be doing, you can put a stop to it by doing nothing more than telling the people. However, don't ever count on it being this simple.

FIND AN ACTIVIST LAWYER

If you find yourself embroiled in a battle as a result of what you have printed, and everyone is angry, it is then time to print more about what is going on. Print what people are saying to you, good or bad. Don't use names of private citizens, just print what is being said. Print letters to the editor, and make sure they are not libelous. I have already explained this to you in another chapter. You need a lawyer in your activist group who will advise you on these matters. If you plan on getting down and dirty, then know what you are doing. You can be sued for telling the truth if it's defamatory. Go to the law library and look it up. If you want to protect yourself, talk to your local insurance man and buy libel insurance. Maybe you have an insurance man in your group.

If you are going to put out a paper, you need many sources. As I said in the chapter on pamphleteering, never disclose sources, or you will be a marked person. Never give out any information on sources, especially if you live in a smaller town.

If you live in California, the Constitution of the state, Article 1, Section 2 (a) & (b), reads as follows:

CONSTITUTION OF THE STATE OF CALIFORNIA
ARTICLE I
DECLARATION OF RIGHTS

SEC. 2. (a) Every person may freely speak, write and publish his or her sentiments on all subjects, being responsible for the abuse of this right. A law may not restrain or abridge liberty of speech or press.

(b) A publisher, editor, reporter, or other person connected with or employed upon a newspaper, magazine, or other periodical publication, or by a press association or wire service, or any person who has been so connected or employed, shall not be adjudged in contempt by a judicial, legislative, or administrative body, or any other body having the power to issue subpoenas, for refusing to disclose the source of any information procured while so connected or employed for publication in a newspaper, magazine or other periodical publication, or for refusing to disclose any unpublished information obtained or prepared in gathering, receiving or processing of information for communication to the public.

Nor shall a radio or television news reporter or other person connected with or employed by a radio or television station, or any person who has been so connected or employed, be so adjudged in contempt for refusing to disclose the source of any information procured while so connected or employed for news or news commentary purposes on radio or television, or for refusing to disclose any unpublished information obtained or prepared in gathering, receiving or processing of information for communication to the public.

As used in this subdivision, "unpublished information" includes information not disseminated to the public by the person from whom disclosure is sought, whether or not related information has been disseminated and includes, but is not limited to, all notes, outtakes, photographs, tapes or other data of whatever sort not itself disseminated to the public through a medium of communication, whether or not published information based upon or related to such material has been disseminated. [*As amended June 3, 1980.*]

UNPREDICTABLE

Never be too predictable, so no one ever knows where you will attack next. Some of the nicest offhand compliments I ever received from people in government were comments like the following: "We were in a meeting the other day discussing an issue, and someone said, 'I wonder what Metzger will write about this in his paper,'" or "One thing you do, Metzger, is keep us looking over our shoulder." I can't think of nicer compliments, because that was always my main goal. I didn't like going around finding fault with government, but it was my job. I didn't really have to go around looking for problems in government; they came to me on a weekly and sometimes daily basis. In my mind, being an activist has more to do with exposing government activities than it does trying to change things the way you think things ought to be changed. Once you become effective as an activist, pamphleteer, newspaper publisher, etc., etc., you then have an even greater responsibility to use very good judgment in how you use the influence you have and not abuse it.

DON' GET COCKY

There were times I felt cocky after winning a long, hard-fought battle. I would take a drive to one of our many old cemeteries and look around at all the grave markers. It was interesting to read the inscriptions, which led one to believe that herebelow laid a once important person. And guess what, folks? The world kept right on going, no matter how important they thought they were. If reading this book encourages people to become politically active and effective, I would hope they always let the Constitution be their guide. If the Constitution is your pilot and you interpret it properly, you will not trespass on another person's rights, will you?

There is another possibility that will give you some experience. Ask your local newspaper if they will buy well-researched and written stories from you. Of course, this is after you have written quite a few letters to the editor and they have published them. The object is to get out there and get good, positive exposure any way you can get it.

Freedom of the press is useless when people do not understand what they are reading.

—*Gerald F. Liebermen*

Please remember this when you write.

"Our Republic and its press will rise or fall together. An able and disinterested, public-spirited press . . . can preserve that public virtue without which popular government is a sham and a mockery."

—Joseph Pulitzer

CHAPTER **57**

Letter Writing by the Numbers

THERE ARE LETTERS to the editor, and there are letters. We are now talking about letters to your elected officials and department heads. I told you before, but I'm gong to tell you again, don't get into battles with government employees. If you have a problem with them, and you believe what they are doing is a problem to other citizens, go directly to their bosses and let the bosses deal with the problem. Rule one, aim your attack in the right direction. I can't emphasize how important it is to think several moves ahead of yourself. Try to calculate in your mind what your opposition is going to do and then proceed, but have a counter-attack already in mind.

ANSWERING BEFORE RESPONSE

On several occasions I can remember writing a tough story and at the same time writing my response, because I knew the kind of response I would be receiving from the opposition. I used to tell my wife I did this so, in case something unforeseen happened, I would have next week's article ready to go. Believe me, when you fight enough battles against some of the same people, their responses are very predictable—just as what you will do will become predictable to your opponents. Keep this in mind and see what you can do to become unpredictable.

Now back to the letter writing. The kind of letters to write to elected officials and bureaucrats when you want some answers is by the number. The following is an example of what I'm talking about.

SIMPLE SAMPLE LETTER

Dear [salutation]

At the last public meeting on 1/1/11 at 7:30, on the issue before the (name the public body), you voted yes on item #12 concerning adopting a new ordinance which will restrict people from painting their house the color they choose. Following are some questions I would like answered. PLEASE number your answers to correspond to my questions so there will be no confusion.

#1. Why did you vote yes on this issue?

#2. Where is the money going to come from to enforce the law?

#3. Is the law going to be strictly enforced, or will it be selectively enforced?

#4. Who is going to decide what color a person can paint their house?

#5. What qualification does this person have to make these decisions for me?

#6. Do YOU think this is a violation of citizens' rights to life, liberty, and property?

#7. Do YOU think this is a violation of your oath of office?

SHORT AND SWEET

The object here is to ask short, to-the-point questions. Numbering them forces them to answer each question. Politicians love to slip, slide, and dance all around the issue without giving an answer. In this format it is rather difficult for them to do this. When you receive their response and find they ignored your request, send back to them a copy of your letter and ask them again to please number their answers. Some people in government just hate having to respond this way, because they are use to sending back a form letter thanking you for your letter. Some of them, after receiving back my letter for a third time, finally realize I'm not going away. They finally cave in and make an attempt at trying to answer my questions, answers containing as little commitment as possible. They know their answers can and do come back and bite them in the ass.

WATCH THE BUZZ WORDS

Today the art of being a good politician is to talk and never say anything, or to try to dazzle you with buzz words and buzz phrases. Read Chapter 31 in the *Wee Wee* book. When you receive a response to your letter filled with buzz words you don't really understand, make a copy of their letter and highlight all the buzz words. Send it right back and ask them to define each one of the buzz words so you will know what it is they said. You can never be faulted for asking legitimate questions, but you can sure look stupid when you try to act like you understand a bunch of double-talk. Keep copies of everything you do—records, records, records.

CC EVERYTHING

Always indicate on the bottom of your letter that you have sent a copy of the letter to other people (in the old days it was carbon copy (cc) to Joe Blow; now we have copy machines). For example, if you write a letter to a county department head about a problem with his department, send a copy of this letter to his boss. If it is really serious, send a copy to the county Board of Supervisors. Send it to the county Board of Supervisors as a body rather than to an individual board member. If you send it to one board member, he or she can file it in the circular file and not respond to you. There is even the possibility that the person you send the letter to might have ties to someone involved and will want to vacillate and waste time so as to reduce the repercussions of your letter. On the other hand, if you send the letter to the entire board, it will go on record, and you will usually get a response. Expect it to take at least two weeks, and longer if the elected body doesn't meet every week. It takes time and patience to deal with government. You can also request your letter be read into the minutes of the meeting. There is then a permanent record of your calling to their attention a certain problem, making it very difficult for them not to respond in some manner.

NO RESPONSE IS A RESPONSE

Many people think that if they don't receive a response to a letter, no one cares. But this is not always true. A no response can also mean they are hoping you will go away. A no response is a response. It is a decision to do nothing, isn't it? If your letter addresses a very important issue, you should send your letter Return Receipt Requested, or hand deliver it and have someone sign stating they received it.

If you are pamphleteering, newspapering, or writing letters to the editor and you are not receiving responses to your letters sent to elected officials, you certainly have all the right in the world to let the general public know that we have some arrogant S.O.B.s in public office who refuse to answer legitimate questions posed to them.

Don't just give them hell. Give them the truth. They will think it hell.

CHAPTER 58

Reductio Ad Absurdum

IN THE *WEE WEE* BOOK I wrote about Frederic Bastiat (Bas-te-a) and his great book titled, *The Law* (1850), and I'm not going to reiterate what I said in the *Wee Wee* book. I am bringing up Mr. Bastiat in this book for another reason. He was a master of a form of logic called *reductio ad absurdum,* which translates into reducing things to absurdity.

PEOPLE WILL LISTEN

This is a very effective way to get people to pay attention. I have used this tactic before, and it does work. It could also be described as cutting the crap with sarcasm. One of the tales told by Mr. Bastiat was used in the 1850s in France when the candlemakers and producers of oil-burning materials were trying to get government to pass a law to protect them from foreign trade. Bastiat, in his light-hearted way, explained in a letter of opposition to the candlemakers' request that maybe the government should pass a law in which all the people should have to cover their windows so as not to allow any light to come into their houses, thereby creating more of a demand for artificial light, which would increase the need for more sheep and cattle to make tallow for the candles, increasing the need for more grain production. In the process we would have an abundance of wool, meat, and leather. This is an example of the kind of logic Horace Mann meant when he said, "False conclusions which have been reasoned out are infinitely worse than blind impulses."

Another example of Bastiat's humor was shown in his example of how to increase jobs in the community in the glass industry: Have someone go around breaking out windows to increase the sales of glass, providing more jobs and thus more prosperity for the entire community.

SELF-INTEREST

At one time a man became very angry with me because I wrote an article exposing the waste in our local government-operated transit system. I used Bastiat's form of logic and showed the absurdity of the entire system. This man was angry because his daughter worked for the transit system—he didn't care that the taxpayers were paying to subsidize the transit system to the tune of almost $6.50 per passenger. The local cab company's average fare at that time was $5.50 per passenger. In other words, the taxpayers could have paid the cab company $5.50 per passenger to haul all the people around town, saving $1.00 per passenger. However, he was only interested in his daughter's job.

SOPHISMS

Sophisms are clever and reasonable arguments that are faulty and misleading. It is kind of like false dilemmas and contrived crises, created by government in order to pass empty legislation for the sake of passing legislation. More stupid logic. An overweight welfare recipient once said on a television interview that it was difficult to lose weight because he couldn't afford to pay for an expensive diet.

You want to know, of course, what this has to do with being an activist. As I tell people over and over, use your ingenuity. Look around your environment. Read the papers, watch the television, and listen to radio, but do it with a critical eye and assume there is probably a biased slant to whatever you hear in the media. Watch for laws your local officials are thinking about passing and try to reduce them to absurdity. Always question everything your local government is going to do. You and your friends are paying for this stuff. Pay attention, show the absurdity of what they are about to do by reducing it to absurdity, and ask them to explain to you what would really happen if they didn't pass the law. Probably nothing.

MR. LOWDERMILK

There was a very creative guy in southern California, Mr. Lowdermilk, who suggested some of the following. Some shallow-thinking bureaucrat suggested a good solution to the street drug problem—eliminate $100.00 bills so as to make it more difficult for drug dealers to carry around their money. To reduce this to absurdity, Lowdermilk said, why not eliminate all paper currency and have the biggest denomination be a silver dollar or, better yet, a quarter. This way drug dealers would have to haul around all their money in wagons. Cops would then just drive around and pick up anyone having a wagon full of money. Or how about making airplanes super safe by building special runways, making it possible for planes to taxi to their destinations. Or why not ban all sharp objects like pencils and pens and make everyone use a computer, so no one will ever get poked in the eye.

DEADLY COMBINATION

Lowdermilk suggested that the greatest danger to the citizens of America is politicians infected with the deadly combination of good intentions and dumb ideas. All you have to do is look around your community and take a look at what you see from a vertical view instead of the normal panoramic, horizontal view. Sometimes you just have to break out of your same old way of looking at things. Live dangerously and think for yourself—think sideways or upside down.

SHEEPEOPLE

People in general have become so accustomed to allowing government or other people think for them, they have become sheepeople. Being argumentative is a good habit to use when you are talking to people. Don't believe everything people tell you. Don't accept everything the government tells you as being the way it has to be. You have a mind; use it. I was raised by an aunt and uncle for most of my childhood. As a kid I remember my uncle always telling me to go into business for myself someday, even if it were selling shoestrings on the corner. By the time I was twenty years old, I was in business for myself and have been ever since. He also told me something more important. Every time I asked him how to do something, he would come right back with "USE YOUR INGENUITY." I'm telling you the same thing. If you want to be an activist you must think for yourself—USE YOUR INGENUITY. The fact you are reading this book says you want to be involved to try to return this government to some form of sanity. If you didn't already realize something is really wrong with our government, you wouldn't be looking for solutions. If you realize there is a problem, you are on your way to finding solutions. I do not have all the answers to the problems you see. I only have suggestions of ways to make your problem-solving easier by following some tried and proven methods of accomplishing your mission.

YOU HAVE A CHOICE

It is your life, and it is your children and your grandchildren who are being sold into slavery. Every day you do nothing is another day they go deeper into debt. They go deeper into debt by the hands of the very people who we the people put into office. Until the people of this country stop thinking government has something to give them or to give to someone who doesn't want to work, nothing will ever change.

Everything evolves around personal responsibility. Since the beginning of time there have been people who are irresponsible, and I imagine there always will be. So what is the solution? Should we all be irresponsible? Should we all quit working because our backs hurt, we're stressed out, our car won't start, and our alarm didn't go off, so we won't go to work today? Should we all quit working because we don't feel good or we can't find a baby-sitter? Or how about staying home to take care of our kids, going on welfare, and letting other working people take care of us? Why don't we all just quit work and go on welfare? This sounds like a good solution. I need a vacation after working for forty years, never missing a day's work, and never having a two-week vacation.

INSURMOUNTABLE???

You know and I know that none of this crap is a solution to anything. It is an irresponsible cop-out that irresponsible people use to justify doing nothing. Trying to tackle the job of reducing the size of government looks like it is an insurmountable task, but it is not. It is no different than eating an elephant. If it were cut up into one-pound chunks, frozen, and if you nuked a piece every day, in about thirty-three years you would have eaten a six-ton elephant. All you can do is every day cut out a piece of government fat, and in 3,400 years it will be all gone. If we can get 1000 people cutting at the fat day after day, we will accomplish the mission in 340 years, and so on and so on. If we had enough people, we would have government down to size before I could complete this book. It might be an absurd analogy, but the premise is sound.

THE SYSTEM WILL CHANGE ONE WAY OR ANOTHER

In the *Wee Wee* book, I said this system will change. It has to change because socialism doesn't work. All over the world governments have discovered this. So why are we still heading that direction? Because there are not enough patriots in the right places to put a stop to it—very simple. Your job is two-fold. Seek out the enemy in your

own community, and destroy and recruit more soldiers for the army.
We don't need more sheepeople, we need more thinkers.

*"But Senator, a good statesman is supposed to be familiar with all
the questions," said a member of the audience.*
"I know," said the Senator, "but not with all the answers."

CHAPTER 59

Government Employees

You MIGHT THINK I am overdoing the government employee issue, but it is important, so pay attention. The rule of thumb is not to attack government employees unless there are no alternatives, and this means if their immediate supervisor refuses to solve the problem. Government employees are supposed to operate by the book, and so it should be. The last thing we need is government employees making decisions on their own. This is what most citizens get angry about. They just don't understand why a government employee can't make a decision about simple little problems. If they were allowed to make decisions on issues, guess who would benefit? Gee, folks, do you think it might be their friends? It would be utter chaos. There would be no system to keep government under control. Think about it. It's the pits having to deal with the system as it is now, but it is better than trying to deal with a system like Mexico's, in which everyone in government makes decisions based on how well you grease the palm of the person with whom you are dealing. How would you like that?

ARROGANT S.O.B.

In one of my public battles, I dealt with the arrogant and abusive attitudes of some of the workers at the post office. This was almost thirty years ago, and it was in a small, local post office I had been frequenting for about three years. One day I had had it with their poky asses and nasty attitudes. They made me feel as if I were infringing on their time and I was a piece of dirt under their royal feet. Well, I let loose with a blistering scolding, which netted me a visit from the local P.D.—and a lesson on how to deal with government employees. The way to handle them is first to go to their immediate supervisor. Tell him about the problem, and follow it up in writing. If this doesn't work, then go to the department head. The last step in the chain of command is your elected officials. If this fails, try to get the local media involved. If they refuse to give you space, offer to put in a paid article. I know this sounds like a lot of trouble to go through to solve such a simple problem, but it really doesn't take that long, and it shows you are willing to allow the system to work. As you go through this process, make sure that you keep a written record of every detail. See Chapter 60.

ENCOUNTER OF THE FIRST KIND

One of my first big battles took place in the 1970s, and it involved government employees who worked for the city building department. To make a long, four-month battle very short, I had a bad experience with a building inspector, lost my temper (this is why I now can tell you not to lose your temper), and physically threw him out of my place of business. No one would listen to me, so I had to take the last step. I paid the local newspaper to print my grievances in the paper. It was written as an open letter to the Mayor and the City Council, asking them to look into abuse of authority by the building inspectors. Within a day or two after the article was printed in the newspaper, I received letters and phone calls from other angry citizens having the same problems. But still no one would do anything. So I wrote a rather nasty article, and the newspaper received so much response that they decided to give me space to continue the battle.

BACK-SCRATCHING

I later discovered the newspaper was having similar problems with the building department, so the newspaper was letting me take the heat for something they didn't have the guts to do themselves. Somewhere in this book I believe I told you this can happen, and this is fine. The mission was accomplished.

ALL IS WELL THAT ENDS WELL

The outcome was that the mayor and a city councilman were not re-elected, and the city administrator, head of the building department, and three building inspectors were fired. An added bonus was the removal of the little woman who worked the front counter. She was moved into the back room where she could no longer deal with the public.

So use the system until you are shown what will not work. Then find a way to accomplish your mission doing whatever you have to do within ethical guidelines. Even the super powers of the world have rules of war, which has always amazed me. You have to wonder how they can agree on how to fight a war but can't agree not to fight the war.

Overheard in a Washington office: *"If you are not confused, you're not very well informed."*

CHAPTER **60**

Record-Keeping

WHEN YOU GET INVOLVED in government battles, or any other battle as far as that goes, you'd better maintain good records. Chapter 8 in the *Wee Wee* book is devoted to this subject. Since you probably will have more than one battle going at a time, get yourself a three-ring notebook and some tabbed dividers. Prepare a section for each battle and maintain records. From the day you see a battle brewing, start a chronological log of events—phone numbers, names of people to whom you talk, dates, and also the time of day. Some people think the time of day is carrying it a little too far, but let me tell you, there will be times you wished you knew the precise time someone had called. Make brief notes of what is said in all conversations. A short note of a conversation you had with someone six months to a year ago can spark your memory, and you will be able to recall just about everything that was said.

NOTES AND CREDIBILITY

You will build your credibility just by having your notes. It shows you are meticulous and methodical about what you are doing. There is nothing greater than being in a meeting and hearing your opponent make a statement about something said six months ago. You can open up your notebook, quote the date and time, and set the record straight as to what was really said.

If you are not a socialist by the time you are twenty, you have no heart. If you are still a socialist when you are thirty, you have no brains.

CHAPTER 61

Show Me the Law

WHEN SOMEONE IN GOVERNMENT makes a demand of you, first ask
them to show you the law that gives them the authority. I one time was
stopped by a traffic cop because he saw white tape on my taillights. I
had put this tape on my lights to give them a more customized look. As
soon as he walked up to me, he told me in a very demanding tone of
voice to take the tape off the taillights. Just as quickly and in a
demanding voice, I demanded he show me a copy of the law prohibiting the tape on the taillights. He made a sharp, military about-face and
headed to his patrol car to get the vehicle code book. He was thumbing
through the book as he returned to my car. He continued to thumb
through it but couldn't seem to find the law. There was no law. End of
discussion.

THERE WAS NO LAW

When I returned to my office, I also looked through the code book,
and I could not find anything that would give him the authority to tell
me to take off the tape. So the moral of this little story is, ask, and

sometimes you shall not receive. Code books are available in every state. The vehicle code book is a good one to have. Sometimes you can get them from your local law enforcement or from the library when they sell off their old books. Legal bookstores also deal in new and used code books.

GOOD OLD ANIMAL CONTROL

In our battles with Animal Control, I remember asking them for the code section of the law they were trying to enforce. They told me it was not in the code section; it was their policy. After a few minutes of explaining to them that policy is not law, they had to back off.

THE THREE BLIND JUDGES

I said before that I wasn't going to retell this story, but it is too good an example not to cite at this point. A case we fought for almost two years involved three municipal court judges who decided to even out the case load in the two municourts by arbitrarily deciding to have traffic cops cite the odd numbered tickets to one court and the even numbered tickets to the other court. After looking at the law, we decided they were in fact violating the vehicle code, which states that one is to be cited to the court nearest to where the offense is committed. After persisting for almost two years we proved them wrong, and they had to follow the law and stop issuing tickets on the odd or even basis.

LEGAL LATITUDE

Use some common sense when you demand that a law enforcement officer show you the law—not while in an emergency situation or in the process of being arrested. Go through the process, and then get a copy of the law. I think you will be very surprised at how vaguely the laws are written. It seems they have to be written that way so as to give some latitude in the enforcement of the laws. But it is the latitude given in the interpretation of the law that creates the opportunity for you to be able to argue and debate your interpretation and be heard. Does this make any sense? It seemed to make sense when I thought of it, but I don't know if it came out properly. I want to make it clear that interpretations of the law by judges are reversed all the time. Even the Supreme Court has reversed itself on occasions, so if you get caught in a situation in which there seems to be a misunderstanding of the law, don't assume you are wrong. In this book you are being trained to think for yourself. So think for yourself and, until someone can show you why you are wrong in your interpretation of the law, assume you are correct.

CAUTION IN THE COURTROOM

In the case involving the three municipal court judges, I had a difficult time trying to convince myself that a lay person could be right and the three judges could be wrong. Try this sometime if you want to get butterflies in court. I am not going to get into filing lawsuits on your own and defending yourself in court. There are too many ways to get yourself in trouble, and I don't want to be the one to get you into a jam. There are several books that can give you this kind of information.

I caution you, filing the papers is the easy part. Trying to carry on an intelligent discussion in the courtroom is an entirely different matter, and the opposing attorney is not going to cut you any slack. Your only salvation is if you have a judge who has patience with *pro per* litigants (people who represent themselves in court). Anyway, there are several books published by Nolo Press in Berkeley, California with the express purpose of helping the *pro per* litigants. Three good books are: *Represent Yourself in Court, Everybody's Guide to Municipal Court*, and *Fighting Your Own Ticket;* also *Brown's Lawsuit Cook Book,* published by Desert Publications, Cornville, Arizona.

DON'T GET YOURSELF IN TROUBLE. Study, study, study. Then, before you venture out on your own, ask or even pay an attorney to review what you are doing. If you get to feeling fairly confident filing the paperwork, it would probably pay to have an attorney argue the case in court. In the process of writing this book, between chapters I have been working on a case for my friend and neighbor, who has a problem involving a mechanic's lien placed on his house. We think it is improper that the lien was filed, and if it is proper, we think the law is immoral. I have followed my own advice and have asked our state assemblyman to ask the California Legislative Counsel for an opinion on this issue. We are doing the research and filing the papers *pro bono publico* (for no charge and for the public good), but we are having a young patriot attorney review the papers. He is also going to argue the case in court. If you follow the same path, you will save money, but most of all, you will feel as though you have some control over your destiny. If you have ever had to hire an attorney to defend you in court, you probably remember feeling totally out of control of your life. You had this feeling because you probably had no idea what the attorney was doing. If you have to hire an attorney, insist that you be allowed to do the research in the law library. It will give you some feeling of control.

GOOD EXPERIENCE, BUT

The result of this experience will give you self-confidence, and besides, it is good background for any activist to have in his or her bag of tricks. Also, have your eyes and ears open at all times and build a list of local attorneys who will do some *pro bono publico* work. Believe it or not, there are attorneys who will help for no charge. It is your job to see to it these attorneys get some press coverage for their efforts. There are many angles. Think, think, think.

IF I HAD IT TO DO OVER

Beating up government with its own laws is exhilarating. It is just as exciting as winning any other competitive game. The problem is, if you don't understand the rules, you are at a real disadvantage. If I could change anything in my past, I would have started at a younger age reading and studying in the law library. You're living in a country today that is in total control of your life through laws. In order to protect yourself, it is imperative for you to understand how the legal system works. There is no way for me to transfer the little knowledge I have learned in the last ten to fifteen years. You have to experience it yourself. At times it is difficult to understand the decisions handed down by the courts. If you take the time to look at some of these strange decisions, you will see that in many cases it had nothing to do with the truth. It had more to do with which side was the best manipulator of the facts and technicalities. Even if you can afford to hire the best lawyers, you should work with them and understand what is happening. It's your life.

"Show me the law that gives you the authority or please materialize in documented form the law that gives you the authority."

CHAPTER 62

Protesting

PROTESTING has been used for years by the radical left, but for some reason the conservatives have not gotten the message. There are of course different levels of protesting, ranging from silent to very vocal and physical. I suggest you pick the middle ground. How about silent protesting? If one didn't like what was being aired on television, one could boycott the products of the advertisers by simply not buying them. Next level, write letters to the television stations voicing your dislike for their tasteless programming and let them know you are not going to buy the products of the advertisers. Enclose a copy of the letter you wrote to their advertiser. If you don't feel you are getting any results, you should rally together some of your friends who feel the same as you do and have them repeat the same letter-writing process. Now the television station might have ten to twenty letters to think about.

CONTACT THE F.C.C.

If you are really serious about this project, another interesting situation exists with television and radio. Every five years television stations have to renew their licenses with the Federal Communication Commission (FCC), and radio stations have to renew their licenses every seven years. You and all your friends could write complaint letters to the station and demand that the FCC look into your complaints. Force the government agency in charge do their job. The station has to put the letters in a file to show to the FCC when they reapply for their license. You also should get the address of the FCC and send them copies of your letters, just in case the station loses their copies—you know what I mean. In your letters to the stations, inform them you are going to send a copy of the letter to the FCC. Write to all of your local radio and TV stations and ask the expiration dates of their licenses. This also puts them on notice that someone in the area is alert to the situation.

DO IT IN THE OPEN

When it comes to fighting government, you don't have to be sneaky about what you are going to do. If they have violated their own rules, the deed is done. You move in, expose it, and demand a redress of grievance (First Amendment right). If you are into pamphleteering, then what I have just told you is the kind of information informed citizens need to know.

GET THEIR NAMES

Do everything in writing. I don't know how many times in the last fifteen years people called me about a problem and couldn't even remember the names of the people to whom they talked, let alone having put anything in letter form. Phones are almost worthless except to get the ball rolling. If you are truly serious about activist work, get it together and do it in writing. Send letters Return Receipt Requested or you might as well not send them. Follow up your phone conversations by sending a letter to the person to whom you talked confirming what you and your witness on the extension line heard discussed.

GUN RALLY AND MEDIA BS

In the late 1980s we helped organize a gun rally at the state capitol. The media was very pro gun laws and lopsided. A group of patriots threatened the local car dealers with picketing if they didn't ask the local television stations to at least give some time to the other side of the issue. We actually did get some air time, but stations chopped us up by airing bits and pieces of our information. You have to be very cautious when you are dealing with the media. If it looks like they are against what you are for, you had better think twice before you get on the air and let them make an ass out of you.

The definition of insanity is doing the same thing over and over expecting new results.

CHAPTER 63

Information and Books to Collect

You HAVE TO educate yourself, and you do this by reading. Get copies of your city and county phone books. Most city and county governments have their own in-house directories; if nothing else, they will have lists of the departments and the department heads. Call all the agencies and request a copy of their department policy manual. If it is a small agency they might not have a separate policy, but there has to be some kind of a policy manual somewhere for the employees and agencies to follow. If there isn't, you might have your first assignment cut out for you. If they don't have extra copies, ask for old copies they don't need. But be careful, just use the old manuals to familiarize yourself with how the system works and what is going on.

BUDGET BOOKS—VERY IMPORTANT

The city and county budget books are a wealth of information, and you usually can get one of their extra copies. You also can get a copy of the proposed budgets when they come out. If you want to do something really worthwhile, get a copy of the proposed budget, go to the budget hearing, get up and speak against any increases, and demand they cut the budget ten percent across the board. I have been too busy to attend the entire budget hearings because they last for days or weeks. But in the past, the minute the floor was open for public input, I took the opportunity to say just what I told you to say. They just sit there with their eyes glazed over, act as if they never heard you, and go about spending your hard-earned tax dollars as if there were a bottomless pit.

MY POINT WAS MADE

At least I had my say. This last year something interesting happened. I got up, said what I had to say, and received the same reaction as always. Only this time later in the year they actually had to cut ten percent across the board because they ran out of money. I tell the elected officials to cut ten percent because I know every department of government will find reasons why their budget should be increased. It is up to the public to try to do something about this.

The budget sessions are a good time to try to get a bunch of seniors to attend an all-day session so they can make objections to the spending of more of our hard-earned money. If an important issue comes up in a meeting, a group of seniors can start a phone chain. Have your phone chain pre set so if everyone makes a couple of calls, you can end up with twenty to thirty people showing up at the meeting within an hour.

PEOPLE POWER

Build that list and use your imagination. Make it a point to talk to people all the time. You just never know who you will run into.

FOR REFERENCE

The books and information I'm suggesting are not meant to be read from cover to cover, hour after hour. They are for reference. They stimulate your mind and give you ideas for problems you can go solve. There are bookstores that specialize in selling patriot, free market, and conservative books. I am looking at my book shelves as I write this and will give you the names of books I think will help a person stay focused. As you get involved in battle after battle, you sometimes need to have a battery recharge and reconfirm that you're not going nuts. It also lets you know that you're not alone out there in trying to stop the cancerous growth of government.

ASSOCIATE WITH GOOD PEOPLE

There is nothing better than to read a book written by a well-known person in history with whom you share similar values. You also begin to realize the situations you are fighting today are the same battles patriots have been fighting for years. Eternal vigilance is the price of freedom. I have said many times that there are few certainties in this world, but with some certainty, I can say that the statement, "Eternal vigilance is the price of freedom," is a near certainty. Anyway, check out some of the following books at your local library. The library can help you locate them, and so can most any bookstore.

GOOD BOOKS—GET THEM

The following are good sources of information: *The Law,* by The Foundation of Economic Education, 30 South Broadway, Irvington-on-Hudson, NY. 10533; *Reason* magazine, 3415 S. Sepulveda Blvd., Suite 400, Los Angeles, Ca. 90034; *The New American* magazine, P.O. 8040, Appleton, WI. 54913; The Cato Institute, 1000 Massachusetts Ave., NW, Washington, DC 20001. The Ludwig Von Mises Institute, Auburn, Alabama 36849-5301. Ludwig Von Mises Institute has many good books and a monthly newsletter.

ONE OF THE BEST

If you have not read the book, *COMMON SENSE,* by Thomas Paine, then you must read it and have it in your collection. As a matter of record, it was originally published as a pamphlet in 1776. This book will reconfirm in your mind that people 200 years ago knew very well the hazards of government.

You should also read Plato's *The Republic*. Plato and Socrates 2,000 years ago also understood the problems of government.

There is nothing new, folks. All we need are elected officials who will read history and learn something from it. It seems as though the only thing we learn from history is, we don't learn from history.

Now don't get bogged down thinking you have to go out and buy and read twenty books in the next year. If you do, you will never have time to be an activist and kick government in the ass.

There are five branches of government: 1. Executive, 2. Legislative, 3. Judicial, 4. Permanent Government (bureaucrats), and 5. Lobbyists.

A billion in America and France is a thousand million. In Great Britain and Germany it is a million million.

BILLIONS??

YEAR—2000
DAYS PER YEAR—x 365
=730,000
HOURS IN A DAY—x 24
=17,520,000
MINUTES IN AN HOUR—x 60
=1,051,200,000
SECONDS IN AN HOUR—x 60
63,072,000,000 SECONDS

From the year zero, when Christ died, to the year 2,000 only 63,072,000,000 seconds will pass. I first published these figures in our newspaper in 1989. At that time the *interest* on the federal debt was right at $63,000,000,000.00. So, in other words, if there was a way to have handed out a dollar bill every second, twenty-four hours a day, for 1,989 years there would not yet be enough dollar bills to pay off the interest on the 1989 debt.

Do you realize that if you were given a $1,000,000,000.00 (billion dollars) in one dollar bills and told you could have it if you counted it, it would take you almost 60 years to count it, working 12 hours a day and counting at the rate of one bill every second.

I put this in the book to bring your attention to the fact that a Billion Dollars is a big chunk of change. We hear the politicians, bureaucrats, and the news media throw around billion dollar figures as it it were pocket change. It seems as though one rarely hears the world million any more. The point here is to get you to pay attention to these types of billion dollar statements, and next time you have the opportunity to vote on a money issue or to influence an elected official's vote on a money-spending issue, think about how much a billion is.

CHAPTER 64

Group Power

ACTIVATE THE SENIORS

THERE IS A GROUP of people who need to be motivated and put to work, and they are the senior citizens. When I speak to groups consisting of many seniors, I usually say something like, "The people in their 60s and above are the people who have allowed this country to deteriorate to the level it is by voting into office the liberal, socialist-thinking people." Since I'm in my late fifties, they don't get too angry with me, because they think I'm including myself in that statement.

No matter why or how you motivate the seniors, they are a group who have the time to get involved and should get involved. You can meet them easily in senior citizen centers, and they many times live in groups in retirement centers. Most of them have children and grand-children, so you can appeal to them from this angle. Seniors know many people and can make connections for you. They can do phone work, stuff envelopes, and contribute funds to the cause.

MOTIVATE THE YOUTH

On the other end of the scale are the youth groups. You have to try to fit the project to the people and their ages. A big part of being an activist is having the ability to pick and choose the right people to do the job. After several years of activist work, I maintained a special list of people who I knew would get involved in certain types of projects. Some people will get involved but only if local government is going to do something to affect their businesses or their pocketbooks. Some people will get involved in a battle at the drop of a hat. They will put in their last dollar because they know the battle has to be fought.

Some people will fight like a pit bull if their ox is gored, but when the battle is over you will never see them again. So don't get discouraged if you help someone fight their battle and they later won't help you. This is just the way it is, folks. As long as you know this ahead of time, you can't say you weren't warned. Just grin and bear it. Don't become angry with people because there are not many people who will get off their asses to help preserve another person's rights. If they would just stop and think, they would realize that by fighting another person's battle, it might guard them against the same loss of freedom down the road.

PEOPLE EVERYWHERE LOOKING FOR A LEADER

Keep your eyes open all the time. When you read the local newspaper, watch for groups of people who are fighting a battle. Get yourself aligned with these people, because you will find there are a few people in every group who will want to get involved in other battles. So continue to build your list of people you can count on if you run across a good battle to fight.

Do not try to keep together an organization on a full-time basis. It will take you more time to keep the people organized than if you just pick a battle and pick the people who best fit the circumstances. As a matter of fact, when you have a full-time group, you always have the ongoing problem of infighting and politics. I personally don't tolerate very well this type of time wasting.

I mentioned in an earlier chapter that not all activists are people who go around trying to keep government under control. There are many good activists who are busy working on projects such as organizing neighborhood watch programs in their community or planting flowers around town, etc., etc. All these types of projects are good if you like doing them. There are many groups from which to draw, such as Boy Scouts, Girl Scouts, high school youth groups, and service clubs. There are always groups looking for community service projects in which to participate. Many times service clubs will donate money to a project if it is not political. If it is politically controversial, don't waste your time asking.

Leadership: *A very small boy was trying to lead his big St. Bernard up the road. When asked where he was taking his dog, the little boy said, "I have to see where he wants to go first." This is the kind of leadership we have in America today.*

MONEY BUT NO INVOLVEMENT

Keep a list of the individuals who in the past have donated money to your projects. You will find there is a segment of people who never get personally involved in a battle but are always willing to contribute financially. As you will discover, this can be very important. It does not cost a lot of money to fight battles, but there are times it is vital to spend money on fliers, mailing, etc., etc. One time we were trying to stop a redevelopment project in our community. Redevelopment is one of those projects which is suppose to solve community blight. Well, if you know anything about government, you should know that most every program it creates to solve a problem usually ends up causing more problems than it cures. This you can take to the bank. Redevelopment can take property through eminent domain at market value and sell it at a loss to a big developer who will do what the city wants done with it, such as building a shopping center to increase sales tax to the city. It also diverts tax revenue away from the police and fire departments to pay back redevelopment grant money. This is an explanation, in a nutshell, that would take hours to fully explore.

GET EXPERTS TO HELP

In the process of stopping this government redevelopment project, we realized it was far too complicated for us to try to understand, so by getting business people who were affected by the project to donate money, we paid someone who was very knowledgeable on the subject to come to a special meeting we had arranged with the powers-that-be in our community. When the smoke cleared, we won, and redevelopment went down to defeat. This was after the City had spent over $20,000.00 promoting it. So you see there are times you have to have funds to kick their asses. Government has no business doing these types of projects. Let the marketplace work. We used in the process of winning this battle several of the tactics I describe in this book. Using our newspaper, we printed week after week the facts about redevelopment and made sure we put extra papers in the right spots in order to agitate the business people into action. We used the phone to rally people into action and packed a public meeting with unhappy people. We put out fliers. We televised meetings and the experts we hired kicked their ässes (that's the English pronunciation, please). We crossed over political and philosophical borders because we informed people how redevelopment would effect them and showed them it was in their economic best interests to join in the battle. So you see I'm not just blowing smoke. I practiced what I'm preaching. I believe it is called on-the-job training.

USE YOUR ELECTED REPRESENTATIVES AND THEIR STAFFERS

Stay in touch with the elected officials and their staffers. They also have some interesting possibilities. Keep a list of their names, because they move around from one job to another. As the years go by, you can build a very broad base of people you know in many areas of government just by keeping track of where the staff members are. They are always trying to move up the ladder for power and higher wages. Some are over-aggressive and are fired because they become a threat to the elected officials for whom they are working. As matter of fact, you will discover that the staffers know more about what is going on than do the elected officials. If you are of the same political and philosophical beliefs as your elected representative and his staffers, they can be very effective and helpful.

CHECKING THE POLITICAL CLIMATE

You can obtain a lot of information from these people. They can tell you what is the political climate and whether or not your project will fly with your fellow voters. It is a way of testing the waters, as I have trained you to do, so you'll have an idea whether or not you will be fighting a losing battle. You also must build a trust with these people before they will tell you how they feel about something. Politicians are not going to say anything unless they have a very good idea what the political repercussions are going to be. This is a fact. Off the record it is an entirely different story. When someone says it's off the record, you'd better keep it off the record and not repeat the information. I always found that there is a way to use the information by camouflaging it, making it look like it came from somewhere else. It is very important to protect your sources.

GROUPS, GROUPS EVERYWHERE

There are patriot groups, patriot newspapers, and even patriot computer networking groups. You are probably asking why I don't give out some names. I don't because many of these groups organize for some particular reason only to disband after the mission is accomplished. If you look, you will find them. You can start by going to gun shows. Many patriots attend these shows, and they will give you a name, someone else will give you a name, and so on and so on. Believe me, it is not difficult. Test your investigative skills and use your imagination. Watch for leads from radio, television, and magazines. Certain rallies will be good for leads. Be a bulldog.

> "There is no third system between a market economy and socialism. Mankind has to choose between those two systems— unless chaos is considered an alternative." —Ludwig von Mises

CHAPTER 65

Getting on Local Radio and Television

Most communities now have a local cable television and a radio station. If you have one or both where you live, then by all means go talk to the owner or manager. Ask what you have to do to get some air time. Beforehand call or write the Federal Communication Commission (FCC) and find out what your rights are. Don't be aggressive and demanding. Even if you know they are required to give time, it doesn't mean they have to give it to you, so be diplomatic. Find out for yourself what the FCC rules are. If I remember correctly, they are required to provide a certain amount of public service air time, as do the big stations.

DON'T DO AS I SAY, DO AS I DO

I've done all these things I'm suggesting, but rules do change, so check them out. If you want to try to do a radio or television program,

141

make sure you have no fear of public speaking. If you feel comfortable speaking in public, then keep in shape by speaking at service clubs. They are always looking for guest speakers. Be prepared for opportunity when it presents itself. It wouldn't do you much good to get air time and then blow it.

BONE UP FIRST

If you are going to try to interview local elected officials, get out your trusty tape recorder and do a few practice interviews ahead of time. I recommend you make up some sample recordings of your interview so the person in charge of the station can listen to what you can do. Most stations already will have on the air some type of weekly public service programming. Listen to it, and if there is something you would like to counter, keep in mind that they are suppose to give equal time to both sides of an issue presented on public service announcements. Check this out with the FCC.

EXPECT IT TO TAKE TIME

Almost nothing happens overnight, so lay out a long-term plan with short-term intermediate goals to accomplish the long-term goal. In my first case as an activist, I was working under people but always watching what they were doing. I always asked myself what I would do if I were in charge. I then started a battle here and there as my time would permit. I spent night after night working on a project so it wouldn't take away too much time from my daily work. You don't want to get so involved that you lose sight of reality, and the reality is that most of us have to earn a living. After writing a few articles for a newspaper and learning the power of the pen through pamphleteering and the press, I bought a newspaper.

PLAN YOUR WORK AND WORK YOUR PLAN

This didn't happen overnight. It took ten to twelve years from the time I first became politically active until I bought a newspaper. As soon as I bought the newspaper, I started laying the groundwork for local cable and radio. It took about five years to get on the air because I was so busy producing a newspaper every week. I also was on the ground floor while the cable company and radio station began their operations. I made it a point to know these people, and it paid off. I have been doing political interviews on local TV for seven or eight years, and I did a radio interview show for about three years. Stop and think. All these programs I have done were non-income-producing. I did it for the experience and to be able to reach people. When I was doing all three—newspaper, radio, and TV—I was reaching more people than anyone else in the county.

REACHING PEOPLE—THE NAME OF THE GAME

How do you become effective? You do it by communicating with people. I talked about this in another chapter. When I sold the newspaper, I immediately started writing the *Wee Wee* book. I still do the TV program. It plays every night of the week and has a current potential viewing audience of about 30,000 people. Writing books can reach many people, so here I am writing another one, and I will probably do another one and another one. I'm telling you this to let you know that you must plan your work and work your plan. It is no different than planning a trip from one coast to the other. You plan your route and take off. If you hit a detour, do you sit there, or do you find a way around it? It is the same way with planing a battle you are going to fight. Think about what you are going to do, and don't go off half-cocked.

If you don't have the ear of the media or you are not the media, you might as well go out into the woods and talk to the trees. This is where pamphleteering plays a big role. It fits between a little newspaper and nothing. You have to reach the masses.

Paradox: If it is true, it might be false. If it is false, it might be true.

CHAPTER 66

Interviewing

BEFORE YOU INTERVIEW people, do your homework. Interviews are a very effective way of learning information about your political opponents, but it is like everything else. You have to be prepared. Don't go into an interview unless you have carefully researched your subject. Put together your questions in some kind of order that takes the person where you want to take him. Have ready your very short, to-the-point questions. When I published the newspaper, the title of my interview was "Point Blank," and this is exactly what I did. I got right to the point, printing interviews verbatim. Good English, bad English, stuttering and stammering—it was all there. In this book I mentioned our little Mafioso elected official and his lack of ability to speak in public. About the most he ever said at public meetings was, "I second the motion." Anyway, somehow I was able to get him to do a taped interview. After transcribing the interview, it was so bad I didn't have the heart to print it, but I still have a copy of the interview on tape.

I know there is someone reading this asking himself how does one get elected officials to do interviews with someone they know is out to hang their ass? Well, first of all, as tough as our newspaper was, they always knew I printed the interviews verbatim. If they couldn't handle themselves, it was not my fault.

NO-INTERVIEW INTERVIEW

Sometimes people didn't want to do interviews so I printed a no-interview interview. This is the way it works. You write out the interview and make it very, very incriminating. For instance, if I knew someone was screwing up, I asked my inside sources to tell me every little detail of what happened. I then would print and divulge in the newspaper all this information. Elected officials then read what some of the bureaucrats had done.

TWISTING A LITTLE DEEPER

I also added another twist to the no-interview interview. I put little statements under the questions, such as, "If his eyes start darting back and forth as if he might be lying, immediately ask him the next question." It was a rather no-win situation for the person who refused to do an interview with our newspaper—not very orthodox, but it accomplished the mission. After a few of these episodes, most people decided it was better to take their chances doing the interview than to get their butts kicked without being able to defend themselves. Mission accomplished.

KNOW THE ANSWERS

Most of the time I knew the answers before I did the interview. I didn't care if people were BSing me, because once the interview was printed, the rope was tightened. It is almost impossible to lie to the press, because once an interview is printed someone will always come out of the woodwork and tell the truth. This almost always happens, so to avoid embarrassment, it is best to tell people ahead of time that the interview will be printed. The combination of doing a good interview with well-thought-out questions and printing the interview in the newspaper is deadly. Funny, after a couple of years of doing interviews, it was almost an "in" thing to have been put to the test of being interviewed by Metzger and still have survived. One had to have been interviewed and published to be anybody.

When you interview someone and you are fairly certain they are leaning toward the socialist philosophical point of view, exhaust their beliefs by simply asking them to explain why they believe the way they do. If you ask "why" often enough, they will run out of answers. Be sort of like a kid, always asking why, why, why. When someone answers, "Because that's the way it is," a kid comes back again with, "But why?" Kids don't say "why" to irritate us. They ask because they are going through a learning stage and they truly want answers. Take the same approach when interviewing. If you are interviewing liberal, socialist thinkers, tell them you really want to understand the liberal philosophy and ask them to explain in detail how it works. They can explain it to a point but then will run out of logical responses, at which point they'll start daydreaming and commenting about how nice it would be "if." History is on your side on the subject of socialism. Never has a socialist form of government survived the test of time. The free market has flaws, but it has worked since the beginning of time. The free market is not a system per se. It is what you get when government does nothing to prevent it.

PROVIDE THE FORUM

I was always fair and right to the point in my interviews—no BS. If I asked the right questions, the people I interviewed did a good job of sticking their foot in their mouth without too much help from me. All I did was provide the forum. There were many people who didn't particularly like me but had a certain amount of respect for what I did because I was accurate. This is a very important point for you to remember. Don't go off half-cocked.

Harry Hopkins, right-hand man to Franklin D. Roosevelt, said, "Elect, elect, elect, tax, tax, tax, spend, spend, spend—the people are too damn dumb to understand."

CHAPTER 67

Stick-to-it-tiveness

WHATEVER BATTLE you choose, it is very important for you to have the intestinal fortitude to stick to it until you have accomplish your mission. If you don't think an issue is important enough to follow through, then don't start. It is a matter of credibility. There's that word again. Please believe me, building your credibility is the highest priority if you are ever to be effective in your role as an activist. Once people know that you will take your battle to the end and prevail, two things happen: first, your supporters will be more willing to get involved in most any issue that you uncover and decide to battle; and second, your opponents will be willing to take a real hard look at the issue you are bringing to the forefront and will try to solve the problem before it becomes a full-blown battle.

THE LONG AND SHORT OF IT

After a couple of years of publishing the newspaper and having made my point on quite a few issues, I remember an elected official saying to me after a public meeting, "You always come in here telling us what you are going to do; we don't believe you, and then you go do it." We worked on battles that lasted for two or three weeks and some that lasted for over two years. The only battle we were unable to complete was cut short because we sold the paper, and it was one of those battles that probably never would have been over. It is sort of like our local Animal Control. We would win a battle, and six months later they again would be doing the same thing. The county legal beagles would bail them out time after time. There are times you would like to throw up your hands in disgust, buy a motor home, and travel or go live on a desolate island in the middle of the ocean. But if you take that route, you would perpetuate more of the same type of crap that has gotten this country in the mess it is in now. There is no running or hiding from government today. It is everywhere, and it starts right in your home town. Pay attention folks.

MUST SACRIFICE TO WIN

Understand that very few things in government change because of a phone call or a letter. It requires a combination of the activities we are talking about in this book. If you don't have the tenacity to make things happen, then don't even start. Think back at the times you have heard young Olympic gold medal winners tell about all the sacrifices they had to make and the hours and years of training they had to invest to become a winner.

I guess the general public of this country will not get off their knees and on their feet until they are bankrupt from over-taxation and made slaves by over-regulation. Will you?

Blind obedience and the fear of government is the author and agent of despotism.

CHAPTER 68

Personal Responsibility

"Personal responsibility" by all citizens could make a real difference in this country. During a radio talk show, I said something about the socialist, utopian daydreamers, and a caller came on and asked me what I would do to change things. My response was to make people be responsible for themselves. I then threw in a definition of the word "responsibility" that I had seen years ago in an old dictionary. It said, "being responsible for that which you are responsible for." The caller came back with, "Isn't that a utopian daydream also?" His question took me aback for a moment, but I then said, "You're right, it is a utopian daydream, but one worth striving for; I can't say that about the socialist utopian daydream."

GOOD POINT, BUT

He made a good point about my statement because all the people in America are not going to become responsible people. There have been irresponsible people since the beginning of time, and I imagine there always will be. We need to motivate the good, responsible people to become activists so they can help reduce the size and power of government. And the good people must demand that the bleeding-heart, no-logic, shallow-thinking utopian daydreamers, who have been in control of this country for fifty to sixty years, stop pushing their agenda onto the public's back. We can no longer afford the tax burden of supporting irresponsible people who want something for nothing.

WHO IS HANDICAPPED

As long as I see people going to work in a wheelchair, then don't tell me that healthy, able-bodied people should be getting free hand-outs. There is nothing that lights a fire in the souls of hard-working taxpayers more quickly than seeing young, long-haired, tanned, dressed-in-shorts shoppers at the grocery store paying for their steak and ice cream with food stamps.

FOOD STAMPS

In California the food stamp program is separate from the welfare department, so check it out in your state. In the state of California, food stamps are given out through the Agriculture Department. Go check them out once in awhile, and see what they are doing. Pretend you own the county and all the agencies and you want to know how your money is being spent. Have the attitude that it is at all times your duty to keep an eye on your government, and it is your duty to do something about it when you find a problem. In other words, become a real pain in the ass.

VOLUNTEERISM

Some people have lost the desire to help by volunteering. Today, the strong arm of government is taking money out of your paycheck and forcing you into contributing. Sadly, you are forced to contribute to programs with which you may not agree. Sadder yet, because we are forced to contribute, we lose the desire to give to worthwhile charities in our own communities or to volunteer our time.

As part of your activist training, you should try to give some time to whatever you consider worthy causes in your community. It shows you're sincere in your concerns for your community and it will help you build more contacts.

You also should pay attention to some of the causes to which you are forced to contribute. Maybe you can expose some of these activities to the public and help put a stop to them in your community. This is a touchy area, so be careful. There will be plenty of bleeding-heart, coercive liberals who helped get these programs started, and they will fight tooth and nail to keep them going—with your money.

HOT ICE CREAM

The socialist, utopian daydream is like asking for hot ice cream. The utopian dream of asking people to be responsible is like asking for meat and potatoes.

CHAPTER 69

Wealth of Information

THE COUNTY AND CITY purchasing departments are a wealth of information. The budget books, the law library, and all these areas of information I'm telling you about are open for public scrutiny. I don't mean that you can go in and browse through the file cabinets without permission, but with permission you sometimes can. If anyone tells you that you can't have certain records, ask them to show you the law prohibiting your right. Also familiarize yourself with the Freedom of Information Act. If an agency doesn't give you information that you request, you have the option of filing papers through the Freedom of Information Act.

PURCHASING DEPARTMENTS

We tracked many purchases through the purchasing department. We learned the county was buying cars out-of-county when they could have saved money by buying them locally. Sales tax also would have stayed in the county. We caught them buying office furniture out-of-county without getting a bid from local merchants. We were instrumental in getting a four percent preference for local bidders, meaning that if a local bidder were four percent higher than an out-of-town bidder, he would still receive the order. We caught the purchasing department abusing the maximum-purchase-without-bid cap, which was $10,000.00. This meant that they could make purchases up to that amount without obtaining formal bids. They were buying items out of the county and writing purchase orders for $9,999.99. This was not illegal but immoral, and they were called on the carpet for it. The different county agencies who used food products were all buying from different suppliers, instead of combining their purchasing power to get better prices for the taxpayer. We changed that. It is a matter of making it your business to know what is going on.

BUDGET BOOKS ARE GREAT

The budget books are a great place to look for expenditures that look out of place. After looking at the books of your government for a period of time, it is easy to spot out-of-place expenditures. Ask any auditor who checks the books of big companies how easy it is to spot discrepancies. Look for big amounts of money, trace where they are going, and check for money lumped under "discretionary" or "miscellaneous." Request they give you a breakdown of where all the money is going. They have to account for every penny, and it is all public record. At all times keep your local government on its toes and never let them know where you will strike next. It was a joke among people who knew me. Whenever they saw me nosing around they would say, "Metzger is trolling again, trying to catch a big fish." They were right. If I trolled long enough, some sucker would bite; we'd set the hook and reel them in. You have to use your imagination on these endeavors. Once you have discovered an illegal or immoral government activity, there is a certain procedure to take once the hook is set. Make an offer to negotiate (they fix the problem willingly). If they won't negotiate, expose whatever you have discovered by whatever means you have at your disposal—letters to the editor, letters to officials, newspaper articles, pamphleteering, radio, television, etc., etc. Hang on and don't let go.

LAW LIBRARY

If you ask for a copy of the law that gives someone in government the authority to do what they are doing, and you have a difficult time obtaining it, go to your local law library. Ask the law librarian to help you look it up. Go to the law library as much as you can. Become familiar with it so you can find your way around. It is very complicated, so don't get discouraged if it takes you a year or so to feel comfortable. Be prepared to do a lot of reading and researching. We are fortunate in our library to have someone who is always willing to help.

If you plan on fighting a battle which involves a particular law, make it your business to read and understand the law. All laws are to be written in easy, understandable language. To the lay person they may seem vague and ambiguous. There are many laws that seem overly complicated, but they are on the books so you must read and study them. It's like a foreign language when you first begin, but you must try. Everything in this country evolves around law. This is a country of law.

LAW DICTIONARY A MUST

One of the handiest tools you can have in your personal library is a copy of *Black's Law Dictionary*. As a matter of fact, it is a necessity when you are reading any type of legal document. Some laws are written with the legislative intent of the law as a preface to the body of the law. Laws generally are written in the broad sense and not written for literal interpretation. This is why problems arise. Someone in law enforcement interprets the law one way, the public interprets it another way, and the courts have their interpretations. If laws are too vague and ambiguous and become a violation of due process of the law guaranteed by the Constitution, then adjustments have to be made, such as appeals to higher courts, where ambiguities will be clarified.

The best example I can give you is one I wrote about in the *Wee Wee* book concerning Animal Control's picking up animals without having a prior hearing. This was a violation of due process of the law, and they had to rewrite the ordinance to comply with the Constitution.

I'm pleased to say that our newspaper was instrumental in causing this change to occur.

DUMPSTER DIVING AND GARBOLOGY

There actually are people who call themselves garbologists, and they are paid to secure and rummage through people's garbage. It's astonishing what one can learn from going through someone's garbage. At this point, I am going to insist that you use your imagination on how you will use this tidbit of information.

Dumpster diving involves the same technique but is usually associated with agencies. Know what I mean?

I don't know whether or not I should be giving away these little tricks of the trade. Oh, what the hell. By putting these ideas in print it could dry up some good sources. Well, it's too late now.

Why is it that the people (socialists) who most believe in the concept of majority rule in politics are mostly against it in the marketplace?

CHAPTER 70

Courts and Juries

W<small>HEN YOU DECIDE</small> that you are confident enough to take on the court system, you had better ease into this carefully, because you are dealing with the pros and sometimes cons. Judges DON'T EVER like to admit that they made an error, as in the odd or even case, Chapter 8 in the *Wee Wee* book and Chapter 54 of this book. Of all the areas in government, these are the people who are the haughtiest of all—and I am not just talking about the judges, I'm talking about the entire crew in some cases. You noticed how I diplomatically said, "in some cases." As I always say, there are no certainties so we always have to speak in generalities. There are, of course, many nice, down-to-earth people who work for the court system.

SOMETIMES IT DOESN'T PAY TO BE RIGHT
WHEN GOVERNMENT IS WRONG

Judges, it seems, think they never have to justify anything they do. A patriot attorney in our county was thrown in jail fourteen times, mostly for contempt of court. He tried to explain to judges they were in error, and the judges became very angry. Thinking he was right, the attorney said that he would rather go to jail than cave in. The attorney proved he was correct in every case, but the system got him in the end. He was disbarred for his actions, so the moral of this story is, it doesn't pay to be right when government is wrong.

STUPID LOGIC—WHAT CAN YOU DO???

On one occasion, we asked a clerk at the courthouse for her signature to confirm delivery of certain documents on a certain day. This person refused to sign and told me to send it certified through the mail. I was thinking, here I am standing in the courthouse, trying to deliver a document, and they want me to drive four blocks and pay the post office to deliver back to the courthouse the very same package, and then they will sign for it. This was ridiculous! I naturally wrote a letter to the presiding judge, told him the story, and asked him to straighten out his employees. He told me that he didn't want his employees signing for documents over the counter. I explained that they have to sign over the counter for certified mail brought by the mailman. He then pulled the power trip on me and stated that's the way it is, and that is the way it is going to be. End of discussion. In this case I didn't think it was worth the trouble to fight it, because they answer to almost no one except God herself. Judges have more discretionary power than any other elected officials, including the President of the United States.

THERE IS ALWAYS ELECTION DAY, THANK GOODNESS

If you run into a judge like this, there is always Election Day. If you get down and dirty during the campaign and you ever have to appear before that certain judge, you can have him disqualified in order to insure a fair hearing. Be cautious, but don't fear them. They can be hurt by the political pain of not being re-elected, just as any other elected official. There are many judges who are not re-elected. They then have to get back into the trenches just like the rest of the lawyers who practice law for a living. Believe me, they don't like losing elections. The only real difference between judges and the rest of the government employees is judges go to work in black dresses. Please, please, any local judges who read this, I am just trying to earn a living writing a book and throwing in a little humor—(as if they will believe that).

JURIES, JURY NULLIFICATION, AND FULLY-INFORMED JURY

Most of you, I am sure, have not been involved in these areas, and I'm not an authority on the subject. So, right off the bat, I'm going to give you a name and address of the group, "Fully Informed Jury Association" (FIJA): FIJA, National HQ, P.O. Box 59, Helmville, MT 59843. As you become more involved with the activist movement, you will begin to realize that this is a country of law. The problem is, there are laws, laws, and more laws. A to-the-point explanation of the fully-informed jury idea is to have intelligent, informed juries who understand that they have the right to judge the law, as well as the facts of the case before them.

MAINTAINING OUR GREATEST POWER

It's a battle to try to make sure that judges inform jurists that they have a right to know this when they sit on a jury. You must understand, the jury is our most powerful tool to hold government to the principles of the Constitution. They can find a verdict in direct opposition to the directions of the judge in the courtroom. The best example of this is prohibition. It was obvious that the people of this country were going to drink alcohol, no matter what the law. If someone went to court for drinking, and the jury found this person not guilty because they thought the law unjust, that law from then on would be unenforceable.

VOTE YOUR MIND

You cannot be punished for voting your conscience, even if you have sworn to follow the law as given. This is a very broad definition of jury nullification, but it should start you thinking. Since we are a country of law, this is a very important issue. Just think, if we had enough informed people on juries, they could make mincemeat of many of the stupid laws on the books.

If you know anyone who is going to be on a jury, contact someone from FIJA. Obtain a thorough understanding of jury nullification and fully-informed juries. With this knowledge, try out your protesting, picketing, and pamphleteering skills. After you know what you are doing, try handing out pamphlets to people reporting for jury duty, explaining what a fully-informed jury is. DON'T DO IT INSIDE THE COURTHOUSE. You might want to ask permission from the presiding judge ahead of time so you won't get in trouble. There was a case in northern California involving a woman who tried to hand out material, and the powers-that-be tried unsuccessfully to prosecute her. Write FIJA. They will know of the case. If you are serious about being involved, you must subscribe to some of the newsletters put out by different activist groups. I'm hesitant about putting too many names and addresses in this book because these groups tend to move around and they come and go, but once you are connected to the underground movement, you will find more groups than you have time for. But it is important that you get an idea of what is out there and align yourself with those who serve your needs. Maintain records of as many as you can get your hands on.

GRAND JURY

A really powerful tool in every community is the grand jury, and it is comprised of local citizens. Anyone can apply and request to be appointed to the grand jury. The presiding judge is usually in charge of the process. In our county there are more people selected than appointed. The appointments are selected randomly by a drawing. This way no one, not even the judge, knows for sure who is going to be picked.

Even if you are not a part of the grand jury, you can use the power of the grand jury by writing letters to the grand jury foreman and asking him to look into problems in government that you think need to be addressed. The main purpose of the grand jury is to be a watchdog of government agencies. But don't be too surprised if they are not real tough in their decisions. A good activist is also a watchdog of the grand jury. A good activist is a watchdog of everything that goes on in one's community. We printed several scathing articles about our grand jury and its lack of aggressiveness in its investigations of certain cases. Don't be afraid to tell them what you think about their reports. Each group of citizen jury members is appointed for one year. Everything they do is done low profile, and if you testify, it is done in confidence. This is an important area with which to become familiar.

Never blame a mirror for what it reflects.

MINI
GRACE COMMISSION

CHAPTER 71

Mini-Grace Commission

I FIND IT DIFFICULT to believe, but there are many who have never heard of the Grace Commission Report of the early 1980s. Then-President of the United States, Ronald Reagan, asked J. Peter Grace to conduct a survey of government agencies to try to find ways of saving taxpayers' money. The survey was paid for by the private sector, zero cost to the public. There were 161 volunteers from top corporate, academic, and labor positions all across America. These people were assisted by more than 2,000 other volunteers. It cost the private sector about 75 million dollars in time, money, and materials to conduct the survey. The end result of the survey was 2,478 cost saving recommendations that could result in a cost savings of $424,400,000,000.00 (billion) over a three-year period. You probably already figured out that the bureaucrats and the politicians as of yet have not adopted very many of the recommendations. None of them want to give up any of the pork in their home districts or take a chance on not being re-elected.

161

CHOOSE A LOCAL PROJECT AND BE EFFECTIVE

Well now, does this give you any food for thought? Are the wheels turning, and are you thinking about getting into government agencies in your community and nosing around? Well, you can start at your local level by first obtaining a copy of the budget for whatever agency you would like to pick for your first project.

THEIR COST AND TRUE COST—NOT THE SAME

Our local transit system is a good example of a good project. Every year they produce a report, and every year I took the report and printed the items they left out. They omitted some rather important items.

They would show their figures, and then I would show the same figures, adding all the items they should have included but didn't. They included items like fare box revenue as revenue, when in fact it was revenue paid through some other taxpayers' subsidy. They also did not include items like insurance, and they didn't amortize the cost of their busses and cabs, which amounted to several hundred thousand dollars. You see what I mean? These are just a few incidentals that they don't include which give the taxpayers an untrue view of the cost of their operation. But you see, the transit is supposed to be of such great benefit that we are suppose to overlook the cost. This is the true socialist way to do business, or should I say to do charity. The point is there are many of these types of boondoggles around for you to expose. Just be alert (America needs lerts).

THE PROJECTS ARE WAITING FOR YOU TO CHOOSE

You could pick any number of agencies on which to do your own little Grace Commission Report. They are there waiting for you to investigate. After you gain some experience, you will find that it is fairly easy to do. Just be willing to invest the time it takes to learn the tricks of the trade. The knowledge you gain will be useful the rest of your life in trying to control government, because it is never going to go away. It will never be as efficient as the private sector because there is no competition and no profit motive. Don't become discouraged if you can't make big changes. This system has had 200 years to evolve to this point, and it is not going to change overnight. You have to have stick-to-it-tiveness or tenacity and that bulldoberman mentality. You have to know in your heart that what you are doing is what it is going to take to return this country's government to some form of sanity. Don't allow anyone to tell you that what you are doing is a waste of time. Those kind of people we don't need. They are part of the problem. Believe me, in the last fifteen years, many people told me I was wasting my energy publishing a newspaper for which I received no financial reward. All I can tell you is, no one can ever say that I didn't give it my best. I have a scrapbook full of memories and evidence that I can pass on to my posterity showing that I did something to try to pass on freedom. This is what it is all about, folks. If you can sleep with yourself doing nothing, then so be it. I can't.

DON'T FORGET THE PROFIT SECTOR

If you start working on a department that could be subcontracted to the private sector, as part of your investigation ask someone in the profit sector to give you a ballpark estimate of the cost of the particular job. If it sounds halfway feasible, obtain a couple of more firm bids and present them to one of your elected officials. Ask them if they are interested in looking into it. If so, rally a few more people and write a few letters to the editor. If you want to get real serious, put out a few pamphlets showing all the facts and figures. Make sure that you are accurate on your figures.

Government regulations cannot change the economic law of supply and demand. All they do is cause it to function in the back alleys, underground.

Ballot Box, Etc.

$\mathbb{A}$s WE GO THROUGH LIFE, we are told that the power of the people is in the right to vote. I don't know for sure if there is that much power in the ballot box anymore, but it is a right. More than a right, it is also a duty. But the power of the vote does not just lie in the right or duty to vote. The power lies in the hands of the voters to be intelligent voters. As an activist, it is your duty somehow to find a way to convince people to vote intelligently. This is a big and almost impossible job because there are so many diverse opinions about the functions of government. To uncomplicate it a smidgen, always try to get back to the basics, and don't clutter your mind with state, federal, and world affairs. Don't accept at face value that all the measures that appear on the ballot have to be there. When you are asked to vote yes or no on a ballot issue, the first question to ask is why it's on the ballot in the first place. If the promoters of the ballot cause you to discuss the issue, they have accomplished part of their mission. As soon as you offer your arguments against the issue, then the proponents find a way to counter the arguments. If you are not careful, they will in their persistence eventually have all the bases covered and voters will be convinced to vote for the issue. Try to make the proponents of an issue prove to you and the voters that there is actually a real need for the discussion to take place in the first place.

PROVE PROOF-OF-NEED

In Chapter 36 of the *Wee Wee* book, I mentioned what I described as the proof-of-need report. The object of the report would be to force government, prior to passing any legislation, to prove beyond a reasonable doubt that the legislation is truly needed. They would be required to do this by listing the people whose rights had been violated as a consequence of not having the law, and that by not having the law it would cause blatant violations of individual rights of the people. As a watchdog, it is up to you to question everything.

DEVIL'S ADVOCATE

The older gentleman from whom I bought the newspaper was interesting to watch in public meetings. When it seemed as though everyone was about to agree on a certain issue, he would pop up with some way-out-in-left-field comment, creating a false dilemma or contrived crisis on what would happen if . . . I witnessed many times the proponents of the proposal before a public body fall apart and lose all the ground they had gained because they couldn't come up with a good defense for ideas presented by the old gentleman. He was a master at causing people to see an entirely new picture and viewing issues from an unexpected point of view. You should work at this. It is a very effective tool. Sometimes this technique involves doing nothing more than playing devil's advocate. Try it sometime. After someone believes they have everyone in agreement, pop up in total disagreement to their argument. Or simply ask from where is the money coming to run this new program or to enforce the new law? Be prepared for some dirty looks and some tension in the room.

ON YOUR TOES

It probably seems as though I have gotten off track from the ballot box, but you have to remember that all the issues on the ballot have to go through a certain process. First, it is somebody's idea, then they rally people behind the idea, and then they write a ballot proposal. There is a pro and con statement attached to every ballot measure. Those statements don't just suddenly appear, and the ballot measure didn't just appear. There was a group of activists out there somewhere putting it together. Your job, as a constitutional patriot activist (CPA) is to know what the other activist groups are doing and be ready to counterattack their every move, if needed. Expose to the public what these groups are doing by using some of the techniques I am telling you about in this book.

You and your group can also use the ballot box to try to get issues on the ballot. You can appeal to your elected officials to put the proposition on the ballot, which is the easiest way; or you can qualify it by getting a certain number of registered voters' names on petitions. Check with the person in your community who is in charge of the Election Department for details. It varies from area to area.

INITIATIVE PROCESS

The initiative process also requires a certain number of registered voters to sign petitions to qualify for the ballot. You have to check out these details in your community.

You can be effective by organizing people for or against ballot measures, using pamphleteering, and writing letters. You can be very effective by setting up phone crews and calling voters. In most areas you can buy a registered voter list from the Elections Department. The lists are broken down by parties, making it easier to target the people you want to contact.

LOOKING FOR INTELLIGENT VOTERS

You have heard all your life the statement, "We need to get more people out to vote." In my mind, this is totally erroneous. What we need are more intelligent voters. I know what you're going to say. Intelligent by what standards? And I'm going to say, "By the standards set by our Founding Fathers and the Constitution."

OFF YOUR KNEES AND ON YOUR FEET

A book on political activism could go on forever because there are so many areas to cover. There are creative activists who come up with so many battles to fight that they would need an army to fight all those battles. And then there are the wanna-be activists who just can't seem to find a project. It takes all kinds to make the world go around, and you have to remember that is what freedom is all about. We are all different. Patriots think we have the right to run our own lives as we see fit, and there are others who think they know what is best for us all. Make your decisions involving activist activities based on the premise of individual rights being the highest priority. You don't know what is best for me, and I sure as hell don't know what is best for you. Don't touch anything that doesn't belong to you, and don't use the coercive arm of government to force fellow citizens to do something they don't want to do. Keep your eyes open and your ears to the ground, and be willing to stand on your convictions. Get off your knees and on your feet.

CHAPTER 73

In a Nutshell

ONE OF THE MOST DIFFICULT JOBS in the world is to simplify, simplify, simplify. I hope I have done that with this complicated subject of political activism. If someone asked me what Political Activism is and what one can do as a political activist, and I had to tell them in one paragraph, this is what I would say:

First, do not not get distracted by state, federal, and world affairs. Second, you must educate yourself and understand how your local government works. Third, pick battles you can win and that build credibility. Fourth, know the philosophical beliefs of your elected officials and your political opponents. Fifth, read good books on history.

Good luck in becoming a political pain in the ass!